GEN Z MONEY $ENSE

GEN Z MONEY $ENSE

A PERSONAL FINANCE AND INVESTING GUIDE

ELLA GUPTA

NEW DEGREE PRESS

GEN Z MONEY $ENSE

A Personal Finance and Investing Guide

ISBN   978-1-63676-943-1   *Paperback*

           978-1-63730-009-1   *Kindle Ebook*

           978-1-63730-111-1   *Ebook*

Contents

Foreword by Neale Godfrey

———

When I created the topic of teaching kids about money in 1988, I could only dream I would someday be passing the mantle on to bright, young people like Ella.

While I was the president of The First Women's Bank in the 1980s, I saw women struggling with money and the concept of financial independence. My research showed that it was because we were never taught anything about money when we were young. I went to look for books to teach my own young children about money . . . and there were none. My three-year-old daughter then quipped, "Mommy, why don't you write the books?" She saw the look of consternation on my face, and then added, "Oh, you are afraid!" I was, but I was not going to let her know. I crouched, established eye contact, and blurted out, "No, I'm not afraid."

From that conversation, the topic of teaching kids (and their parents) about money was born. My goal was to empower generations of kids to dream their financial dreams and to empower them to design their lives in such a way that they would be healthy, contributing members to their families and to society. I'm proud to be a *New York Times* #1 Best Selling Author (with the help of appearing on *Oprah* thirteen times), and I'm about to release my twenty-eighth book.

Over the years I have not only reached millions of kids, but I have also been fortunate enough to mentor many budding entrepreneurs and authors who will speak to their generation about financial empowerment.

I was introduced to Ella by Greenlight, a company that supplies parents with financial tools for their kids. I'm an advisor to Greenlight. During my first phone call with Ella, her brilliance and dedication to the topic of educating Gen Z came across loud and clear. Ella is a voice for your generation.

She understands and can speak the language of Gen Z. Ella recognizes that the members of your generation must learn the consequences of their financial choices. She knows we have not yet been able to totally reach all youth, and teaching financial literacy is a lifelong process. She also understands that the consequences of not being financially literate can be disastrous.

We all strive for independence, but how can you achieve financial freedom without being a master of your own money? You need to understand what money can and can't do. It can't buy self-esteem; it can't buy love. It can't make you happy. These can be tough lessons when we live in a world where making quick bucks seems within everyone's grasp. Learning about money is gaining the understanding to never confuse *net worth* with *self-worth*.

As my generation passes the baton to yours, we encounter the world in which you were born. Your generation doesn't know the rotary phones we had, or remember the period when the princess phone was a revolutionary invention. You are completely immersed in the digital world, which will influence your every behavior. In fact, when it comes to the world of money, hard currencies will be considered relics to be collected like vinyl records. We are moving toward a time where your retina will be your ID, and it will be able to be scanned to complete banking transactions.

Gen Zers have a strong work ethic and want to save money. In fact, studies show this generation is a generation of savers. Over 20 percent had a savings account before they were ten, and 12 percent are already saving for their post-career life.[1] Go Gen Z!

Your ease navigating the digital realm is changing the way we handle and interact with money. Nearly half of Gen Z has a payment app, and only half have visited a bank in the last month. You earn, save, spend, and share from your smartphones.

Your generation wants to talk to and learn from your own influencers. You want to pick a restaurant, a device, and even a mate from a digital source used by your peers. That's why Ella's voice is so important. She is a Gen Zer and can speak with authority to her generation . . . and people will listen.

---

1   Taylor Hugo, "Gen Z & Money," *Thrivent Magazine*.

This book is a must for the Gen Zers who want to grow up to be money savvy. If you want to be in control of your life, you have to be in control of your money. Ella is a voice for you. Enjoy the journey she will take you on to design your financial future.

—Neale Godfrey, chairman and president of the Children's Financial Network, Inc., former executive at The Chase Manhattan Bank, author of twenty-eight novels, contributing writer to Kiplinger, former president of The First Women's Bank, and founder of the First Children's Bank.

Introduction

———

Imagine floating in the Dead Sea with the warm sun shining on your face, relaxing in a pod hotel in Tokyo, or exploring the streets of Madrid on Lime scooters at 3 a.m. while eating chocolate-dipped churros. Over the course of two years, Nate O'Brien traveled to fifteen countries (Austria, Canada, China, England, France, Hungary, Ireland, Israel, Italy, Japan, Mexico, the Netherlands, Panama, and Spain), as well as twenty-nine US states. His favorite part of traveling has been meeting people and forming friendships "in a spontaneous and random manner."

Nate's fantastic life of freedom had humble beginnings. His family rarely took vacations and often camped near their house for getaways. His parents supplied him and his siblings the basics—a roof over their heads and food—but they raised their kids with the mentality of: "If you want something, you have to figure out how to get it." Nate's financial journey began during the depths of the devastating 2008–2009 financial crisis when he was eleven. He had heard his uncle and grandfather casually chatting about the stock market and investing during holiday dinners. These dinner conversations piqued his interest in beginning to invest himself. The stars aligned when a school project required him to learn about the stock market.

He asked his parents to help him open a brokerage account. He then put fifty dollars in it and purchased a share of Cedar Fair stock at a price of around twelve dollars. Every time Nate received money for his birthday or earned small sums of money from mowing lawns and splitting firewood, he added the money to his investment account. Over time, his money grew from a couple hundred dollars, to a thousand dollars, to a few thousand dollars, and has only grown from there. In 2017, he created a personal finance YouTube channel to help others live out their own definitions of financial freedom. Within four years, it garnered over one million subscribers.

Twenty-two-year-old Nate says he is now practically at a point where he could stop working today and retire. He asserts, "Of course, I wouldn't just kick my feet up and laze around all day. [Financial freedom] allows me to work on and build things I am actually passionate about, rather than being forced to work for money."

The story of Nate's success intrigued me. Gen Z is often discounted as irresponsible and financially unaware, but this example indicates otherwise. I wanted to explore whether Nate's life experience was unique or indicative of a larger generational trend. What I discovered has given me cause for hope and excitement.

Gen Z (whose members are deemed Zoomers) loosely includes those born between 1996 and 2010. Although millennials and Zoomers are often lumped together, the times during which we grew up differ. Gen Z was not directly impacted by the Great Recession, but we watched our parents experience the tumultuous time. Then, we watched millennials go through the student debt crisis. These factors have contributed to our generation being inherently financially conservative. According to a survey by the American Psychological Association, Gen Z consumers between the ages of eighteen and twenty-one view money as their top source of stress. In fact, four in five Zoomers name money as the top item in the list of things that "freak" them out.[2] But these fears play an important role in how we choose to manage our money and influence our judicious approach to personal finance.

"THE MOST DISRUPTIVE GENERATION EVER"

A November 2020 report by Bank of America concluded that Gen Z "will be the most disruptive generation ever." In fact, despite lost earnings from the pandemic, our generation's collective income is expected to eclipse that of millennials by 2031. Our income is expected to increase to $33 trillion as we enter the workplace, accounting for over a quarter of the global income. Gen Z's economic power is rapidly growing and is expected to permanently alter the investing landscape. There were a few other findings in the report that stood out:

- Sustainability is an important issue to the Generation Z consumer.

---

2   *Stress in America: Generation Z* (American Psychological Association, 2018), 5.

- The firm predicts environmental, social, governance (ESG) investing will continue to garner a large focus and gain momentum.
- Our generation is open to using new technologies, including robo-advisors and mobile-focused investment platforms, to manage our finances.[3]

In a *New York Times* article, Lucie Greene, the worldwide director of the Innovation Group at J. Walter Thompson, called Zoomers "millennials on steroids." She comments, "If Hannah Horvath from *Girls* is the typical millennial—self-involved, dependent, flailing financially in the real world as her expectations of a dream job and life collide with reality—then Alex Dunphy from *Modern Family* represents the Gen Z antidote. Alex is true Gen Z: conscientious, hard-working, somewhat anxious, and mindful of the future." In the article, Neil Howe, an economist and author of over a dozen books on generations, draws a parallel between Gen Z and the Silent Generation, which he claims was shaped by war and the Great Depression and grew up to be the "diligent" careerists of the 1950s and 1960s. He also points out that the Silent Generation wasn't just the most career-oriented generation in history; it was also the richest.[4]

No generation has had the resources Gen Z is fortunate enough to have right from the beginning of our financial journeys. Gen Z is the most networked generation to date

3   Haim Israel et al., *Thematic Investing; Ok Zoomer: Gen Z Primer* (Charlotte, North Carolina: Bank of America Corporation, 2020).

4   Alex Williams, "Move Over, Millennials, Here Comes Generation Z," *The New York Times*, September 8, 2015.

and has a flow of information at our fingertips. Growing up in the era of technology, our generation has access to new innovations that have made it easier than ever to make saving and investing a habit. These new technologies have given rise to investing platforms that allow us to start investing whether we have five dollars or five thousand dollars. If we learn how to effectively utilize our resources and dedicate ourselves, Gen Z has the potential to become the most financially successful generation ever.

MY STORY

When my parents (both doctors) were just married and completing their medical training in Baltimore, Maryland, they were, as my mother puts it, "dirt broke." They were working eighty hours per week and earning less than minimum wage. One day, my mom was paying bills and she calculated how much money she and my father owed in student loans and how long it would take them to pay off their debt if they paid the minimum dues. What she subsequently discovered made her feel sick, as if she "had just been sucker punched in the gut." She discovered she and my father had well over six figures in student loan debt combined, and it would take them decades to pay it off if they paid the minimum monthly amount. Consequently, she began to learn about personal finance. She started going to the library to read about money management. She realized you have to learn about how money works if you want to make it work for you.

Just starting off in their careers, my parents were the very embodiment of living within your means. They often received comments on their house like, "Aren't you both doctors? Why do you live in a place like that?" However, they were determined to become debt-free. Except for socking away money in a savings account, they contributed the majority of their income toward paying off their student loans.

After several years, they managed to become debt-free. However, they realized paying off the debt was just the beginning. After paying off all their student loans, my parents began investing in the stock market to grow their money. They moved to North Carolina and were able to fund a down payment on a house. By the time I was born several years later, they had designed and built a house. They were able to start a family and create a college fund for my sister and me. Today they live debt-free and in financial freedom.

Since we were young, my parents have instilled the value of money in my sister and me. They taught us the importance of investing in our futures.

When I was ten years old, I visited a Mexican restaurant with a friend and brought my Rainbow Loom bracelet kit with me. When the waitress came over to take my order, she noticed an intricate navy blue and lime green bracelet I had just finished weaving resting on my lap. She asked me if I would sell her one for five dollars. After that night, I began my first business selling Rainbow Loom bracelets. In total, I made around $500 in profit. I invested half of the money in the stock market and donated the other half to a charity close to my heart. By 2021, the money I invested more than quadrupled. I also opened a retirement account at age fourteen after working my first job.

I have been exposed to financial lessons from an early age but realize that so many of my peers have not had similar opportunities. I am now paying forward the knowledge my parents gave me. From a young age, I understood the opportunity cost of every choice and the importance of investing in *yourself.*

However, this book is not just my voice. I have interviewed numerous financial experts, ranging from CEOs to business reporters to professional athletes, who have shared their unique stories, insights, and mistakes with me to pass on to *you.* This is a guidebook for navigating the new world of finance. Reading it is an investment in yourself.

WHY IS THIS BOOK IMPORTANT?

"When will I actually need to know this in real life?" This question has likely crossed your mind multiple times in school when completing assignments that don't seem to have clear real-life applications. However, financial literacy is a basic life skill that actually *needs* to be taught in school. Learning about personal finance and investing is just as important as learning how to drive a car or learning how to swim. Financial literacy has only become more important in the digital age with so much information available and so many new ways to manage your money.

Many people believe more income directly leads to a better financial situation or that it is only necessary to learn about personal finance once they have a lot of money. However, the acquisition of practical knowledge is the difference between those who achieve financial independence and those who do not. It is crucial to be able to understand how to effectively save, spend, protect, borrow, and invest money. Ignorance about such topics often comes at a great cost. Becoming financially literate *now* can save you lots of money in the future, as you can avoid costly mistakes. This book will teach you how to make informed decisions about your money and how to set yourself up for a secure financial future.

Finances play a role in practically every area of our lives. It does not matter how much money you make or have if you are unable to manage it. Unlike previous generations, Gen Z cannot necessarily rely on Social Security or pensions to fund our retirements, making it even more critical for our generation to have an understanding of finance.

Most people think learning about money is a daunting and stressful process. However, I maintain that money shouldn't be a source of anxiety but, rather, one of possibility. You don't have to dissect the *Wall Street Journal* daily or spend your Saturday nights clipping coupons while you eat ramen. This book is based upon the idea that by beginning to pay attention to your finances today, you can form habits that will pay dividends for the rest of your life.

This book includes:

- A discussion on why Gen Z is poised to create massive wealth and the unique way we interact with money
- The basic frameworks of personal finance and investing
- An introduction to new developments in the world of finance that make it easier than ever to meet your definition of financial success

- Financial and investing pitfalls to avoid
- Stories and insights from financial experts

HOW TO USE THIS BOOK

This book is divided into four parts. Part 1 introduces the unique aspects of Gen Z and prepares you for your journey. Part 2 covers foundational financial concepts, and Part 3 discusses the benefits of investing and teaches you how to put your money to work in the stock market. Part 4 contains information on new financial technologies and Gen Z-specific financial trends.

Although I recommend reading this book in order, feel free to skip around to the different chapters and sections according to your needs in a "choose your own adventure" fashion. At the end of each chapter, there will be "Z Notes." If reading this whole book seems intimidating, these Z Notes will provide you with a brief recapitulation of each chapter. However, try not to use them as you would SparkNotes; utilize them to review.

After all, you have time on your side.

PART 1

THE GEN Z REVOLUTION

CHAPTER 1

The Z Factor

———

Lazy, overconnected, addicted to their phones—many people associate these negative stereotypes with Generation Z. However, these stereotypes are far from true.

Generations exist on a continuum, and each generation has unique defining characteristics. Trends exist among different generational groups, ranging from fashion to the role of technology in daily life. Millennials and Zoomers are often clumped together and thought of as one entity. However, just because we are close in age does not necessarily mean we share the same view of the world. Let's dive a little deeper into what makes Gen Z so unique, especially when it comes to money.

OUR UPBRINGING

Instead of being divided by arbitrary dates, generational groups are divided by events. The 9/11 attacks serve as the cutoff event between millennials and Gen Z; it significantly shaped both cohorts but in different ways. Gen Z was too young to feel the emotion and uncertainty of 9/11—in fact, most of this generation wasn't born yet. The general tenet is that Gen Z simply cannot process what the world was like before the horrific attacks.

Furthermore, the Great Recession shaped Gen Z's pragmatic relationship with money. During the crisis, we witnessed how quickly money can dissipate. Although our generation wasn't directly impacted by the recession, it is a reason why many of our decisions are financially driven. Jonah Stillman, cofounder of GenGuru and bestselling author of *Gen Z @ Work,* says of Gen Z, "In our early stages of life, we have been surrounded by a lot of instability and unrest. We came of age in the Great Recession, during which the average net worth of our Gen X parents fell by nearly 45 percent. So, you have a generation that—at a very young age—is acutely aware of saving for the future and preparing for the best and worst scenarios."

The COVID-19 pandemic is Generation Z's defining event. Although the older members of our generation undeniably felt pain as they entered a tough job market devastated by the pandemic, the pandemic fortuitously came at a time when the majority of Gen Z was young and could learn from the crisis rather than be financially derailed. In fact, nearly 60 percent of Zoomers surveyed by *Morningstar* in 2020 were hopeful about their financial lives. These respondents reported feeling high levels of optimism and happiness despite challenges caused by the pandemic.[5] Additionally, a Vanguard survey found that 77 percent of Gen Z decided

---

5   Stan Treger et al., "Dispatches from Generation Z," *Morningstar,* June 2, 2020.

to manage their finances more closely because of COVID-19.[6] Our generation has developed the understanding that circumstances can change in the blink of an eye, which has made us predisposed to frugality and prudence.

TECHNOLOGY

Gen Z is the first digitally native generation. Technology is seamlessly integrated into our daily lives and is not something we struggle to adopt the way older generations do. More connected than previous generations, Gen Z embraces this wide breadth of knowledge at our fingertips. We have been exposed to AI, automation, and mobile platforms from a young age. Take a look at a timeline:

2007—First generation iPhone invented
2008—App store created
2008—Robo-advisors launched
2009—Bitcoin released to the public
2009—Venmo and Square founded
2010—Instagram launched
2012—Acorns founded
2013—Robinhood founded
2019—5G launched

Jonah Stillman and his father trademarked a trait they dub "phigital." Jonah explains, "It's the idea that the physical and digital worlds have pretty much always overlapped, and Gen Z views them as one and the same. For example, whether I

---

6   The Vanguard Group, Inc., *Generational Views on Financial Advice, Investing, and Retirement*, 2.

put something in my cart at the supermarket or click 'add to cart' on Amazon, it doesn't make a difference where or how I get the item if I am getting the same product. That's not the case with other generations. We are digital natives, and we are the first. All of the generation before us were digital pioneers. We are a generation that has never really had to pioneer for technology at all because it has always been a part of our lives."

Gen Z knows a world in which there is a digital equivalent for practically every physical element. However, our generation does not necessarily choose one or the other; it's a union of both. This concept translates to our finances as well. For example, Gen Z has access to both robo-advisors and human financial advisors. Essentially, we are able to use technology as a tool where we see fit.

Our digital world has given rise to the rapid growth of the fintech (financial technology) industry. "Fintech has been completely disruptive," remarks Jennifer Barrett, author of *Think Like A Breadwinner* and chief education officer of Acorns, a saving and investing app with more than nine million users as of early 2021. "In the old days, you had big financial institutions that were primarily focused on more affluent investors because they made more money off them. With a lot of new startups like Acorns there is a more con-certed effort to reach younger and less affluent investors and to open the doors to investing for them. That's huge." To be sure, Zoomers utilize technology to manage our finances differently than our parents do. Iris, a student at Stanford University, comments, "My mom interacts with money dif-ferently than I do. To invest, she uses a computer and logs in to her brokerage firm's website. She's never heard of Robinhood. Investing for me is really easy because I just log into an app on my phone."

Barrett comments, "There's more interest in investing among young people, which I think is a result of fintech companies making it more accessible. For example, Acorns has a program for college students where we waive fees. A lot of people begin to invest with Acorns while they are in university. If you develop those habits while you are in college, there is a good chance you will stick with them afterwards."

Technology is central to the way Gen Z interacts with our finances. The time of physically depositing a check at a bank branch is becoming an anachronism. As we turn to digital platforms like Apple Pay and Venmo, Zoomers have contributed to the decline of cash. Additionally, our generation takes advantage of new services like robo-advisors, which offer rookie investors an affordable, simple way to receive support on their financial journeys.

Technology also shapes our generation's habits as consumers. Online reviews enable us to make meaningful, informed purchases, and blogs that dissect companies and their products allow us to explore what brands really stand for. Forty-seven percent of Gen Z use their phones in-store to check prices and to ask family and friends for advice when making purchases.[7] Moreover, our generation is able to use our smartphones as a means of generating extra cash; it is easier than

---

7   Jeff Desjardins, "Why Generation Z Has a Totally Different Approach to Money," *World Economic Forum*, November 30, 2018.

ever to download an app like Poshmark and sell belongings that are no longer being used.

The easy access to information that has been afforded by technology has resulted in a multitude of financial and investing resources. There is no shortage of personal finance blogs and websites for one to augment their knowledge. Because Zoomers were born into a world with technology, we are comfortable navigating and making decisions within this spectrum.

Lastly, technology allows our generation to stay connected to the world. We are constantly in tune with global news and don't live in a bubble. Unlike our grandparents, we don't have to wait to watch the six o'clock news to learn about world events. Because of the understanding we developed from a young age that the world is unpredictable, we are more likely to make wise decisions about our financial futures.

SOCIAL CONSCIOUSNESS

Gen Z is driving a new normal and creating rippling trends. Many Zoomers are activists and are not afraid to openly express their beliefs. The most diverse generation to date, we create opportunities to discuss international affairs and are not afraid to publicly voice our political opinions. Unlike previous generations, we grew up with an African American president and have always known gay marriage to be legally accepted.

Our generation is blazing our own trails and creating solutions to pressing international problems. In 2019, *Time's* Person of the Year was sixteen-year-old Greta Thunberg, the Swedish activist who created and led a movement of millions as she demanded action in the face of the worsening climate change crisis. Emma Gonzalez and David Hogg, survivors of the 2018 Valentine's Day shooting at Marjory Stoneman Douglas High School, organized the March for Our Lives protest and advocated for gun control laws along with their peers, launching a national movement. In fact, they leveraged social media, popularizing #NeverAgain. Or take Gen Zer Melati Wijsen who, along with her sister, founded a social initiative to eliminate single-use plastic bags in Bali called Bye Bye Plastic Bags. In 2018, the sisters succeeded in their mission to persuade the Balinese government to ban single-use plastic bags. The duo galvanized their community to stage Bali's Biggest Clean Up, an annual beach cleaning initiative which, as of 2020, saw around 57,500 people remove 155 tons of plastic from Bali's shores. They created a global youth movement. Today, they have fifty teams in twenty-nine nations and have spoken about social and environmental issues with world leaders from the United Nations, the International Monetary Fund, and the World Economic forum.[8]

More than any other generation, Gen Z acutely understands that the way things have always been done is no longer good enough. Change is no longer an option but a *necessity*. We understand that if our world is to continue to sustain itself, some old ways of doing things must become obsolete.

How does this relate to our financial habits? Well, in recent years, socially conscious investing options have surged, allowing Gen Z to put our money where our hearts are. Kelly

---

8   Karen Gilchrist, "She Got Plastic Bags Banned on Bali by 18. Now She Wants to Mobilize Other Young Activists," *CNBC*, August 20, 2020.

Lannan, vice president of Young Investors at Fidelity, comments, "Younger generations, including millennials, are very conscious and want to make the world a better place, and that's even more so with Gen Z. The ability I've seen of Gen Z to drive change as well as ensure they are spending their money to align with their values has been amazing." Tiffany "the Budgetnista" Aliche says of Gen Z, "They're 'woke.' I can see them using their money in a way that reflects and aligns with their morals and values."

Gen Z has a penchant for thrift shopping, viewing it as a financially friendly sustainable practice. In fact, a Piper Sandler Taking Stock With Teens spring 2021 survey found that 47 percent of Gen Z has purchased and 55 percent has sold secondhand.

Our generation recognizes that the goal can no longer be to profit at any cost. Rather, it is necessary to profit in a way that aligns with what is right for not only the planet but also for *all* its people.

FINANCIAL AWARENESS

Besides having a gamut of new tools at our disposal that makes it easier than ever to be financially successful, many members of Gen Z have already embarked on a path to financial security.

Lannan says, "Gen Z has been money conscious since they were in diapers . . . in my opinion, more so than previous generations. They are motivated to save their money and also motivated to make their money work for them. A perfect example is the side hustle. Many [Gen Z] folks are already working or are looking for opportunities to earn money and make it work for them."

Credit bureau TransUnion conducted a study examining consumers born after 1995 and their credit histories. Researchers found that over half of Zoomers are credit-active and have a vantage (credit) score of 661 or above, and we aren't struggling to pay off our debt to the same extent millennials did.[9] Additionally, in a TD Ameritrade survey of Gen Zers, 73 percent indicated that they chose or would choose a less expensive college to avoid debt. The financial firm found that Gen Z is on the path to taking on less student loans than millennials. Having little or no debt means we can enter the workforce with mobility and take jobs we really want that may pay less because a large portion of our salary won't be allocated toward chipping away at student loan debt. As of this writing, student loan debt stands at $1.6 trillion, a number that has not gone unnoticed by Gen Z. Because we are connected to the internet, we are familiar with the profound impact that debt can have on our lives and are determined to not be caught unprepared. Sixty-two percent of Gen Z is setting money aside for higher education expenses, and 48 percent plan to work a part-time job during college.[10]

Gen Z is certainly very forward and progressive thinking. The average age Zoomers begin to research financial planning is thirteen, and 89 percent say planning for their financial

---

9   Chloe Anagnos, "When It Comes to Money, Gen Z Is Way Ahead of Millennials," *Foundation for Economic Education*, February 25, 2020.

10   Gabrielle Olya, "How Gen Z Plans to Avoid Student Loans," *Yahoo Finance*, December 3, 2020.

future makes them feel empowered. In fact, as of 2020 (when the oldest members of Gen Z were twenty-four years old), 60 percent of Zoomers already had a savings account and 54 percent had a checking account.[11] Additionally, in a survey, 32 percent of Zoomers reported stashing away enough money in their savings account per month to make them feel confident—a figure nearly 10 percentage points higher than members of Gen X.[12]

What's more, Gen Z is quite pragmatic. Eighty-eight percent of 2017 graduates, the first Gen Z class to graduate from college, chose their major with job availability in mind. In fact, research firm XYZ University discovered that two in three Zoomers would rather have a job that offers financial stability than one they enjoy.[13] This trend is dissimilar to millennials, who have generally been known to prioritize finding a job that has a good work-life balance and that they find fulfilling over one that pays the bills. Of course, this is not to say that if you find a job you love that doesn't necessarily have the best pay, you shouldn't pursue it. This book is meant to teach you how to make your money work for you so you can live the life you desire. The fact that compensation and benefits are a major part of Gen Z's decision-making process when choosing a job simply speaks to our financial awareness as a generation.

---

11 Desjardins, "Why Generation Z Has a Totally Different Approach to Money."

12 Savanna Swain-Wilson, "10 Ways Gen Zs Spend Money Differently Than Their Gen X Parents," *Insider*, November 28, 2018.

13 Desjardins, "Why Generation Z Has a Totally Different Approach to Money."

GEN DIY

"Gen Z is willing to take risks at a young age," says Stillman. "Baby Boomers raised their millennial children under the notion of 'try your hardest,' 'if you work hard, you're a winner in my eyes.' Millennials were given the famous participation awards. The way we were raised by our Gen X parents was very different. It was this idea of work hard or you could be a loser. This idea of competitiveness is very unique to Gen Z."

Gen Z is independent and able to create opportunities for ourselves. Stillman comments, "Gen Z has had pretty much unlimited access to information since birth. We're willing to try things on our own, whether that be learning a new skill like playing an instrument via YouTube or trying to be self-employed in e-commerce."

FATHER TIME

Finally, Gen Z has a unique edge compared to other generations: *time!* As you will learn throughout this book, time is the secret to success when it comes to investing and achieving financial independence.

Our generation's biggest hurdle is a lack of quality financial education.

As of this writing, only twenty-one states mandate personal finance courses. However, a Greenlight survey found that 73 percent of Gen Z want more personal finance education and 86 percent are interested in investing.[14] "Gen Z is hun-

---

14   "Survey Finds Gen Z Lacks Knowledge in Personal Finance and Investing," Greenlight Financial Technology, Inc. press release, April 1, 2021.

gry for money knowledge," says Tanya Van Court, founder of Goalsetter. Luckily, that is what this book is for; it will provide you with all the knowledge you need to embark on your financial journey.

PART 2

A PERSONAL
FINANCE PRIMER

CHAPTER 2

Your Money Mindset

———

"Money is only a tool. It will take you wherever you wish, but it will not replace you as the driver."

—*AYN RAND*

Money makes the world go 'round. Money can be an emotionally charged subject. Everyone has different thoughts and reactions when they hear the word "money." Your money mindset is the unique set of beliefs and attitudes you have surrounding money. It drives your financial decisions.

BREAK THE SILENCE

Many Americans have grown up with the belief that money is one of the few hush-hush topics that should be avoided in polite company at all costs. In fact, studies have shown that parents are more likely to talk to their kids about sex and drugs than about money. But if you want to be in control of your financial life, overcoming a fear of money is necessary.

What are the consequences of not talking about money?

Not paying attention to your finances can have dire ramifications. CFP® Ben Martinek says, "The worst thing anybody can do is neglect their finances and just turn a blind eye to them, to never manage them or control them. It may work out okay, but you will probably miss out on a lot of opportunities, and it will only cost you. When you neglect your finances, that is where it gets expensive." Financial problems are one of the most commonly cited precursors of divorce. Plus, as wage stagnation continues and the wealth gap widens, eliminating the stigma attached to money is critical for igniting change.

Being open about money doesn't necessarily mean divulging your entire financial history to all your friends and colleagues, but it can mean seeking advice and learning from those in similar situations, as well as from financial experts. We live in a society in which a person's social media feed represents a perfectly curated version of their life, for fear of being judged. Many people are afraid of making mistakes and being shamed for financial ignorance. However, being open is the first step to achieving financial success.

Jill Schlesinger, CFP®, CBS News business analyst, and author of *The Dumb Things Smart People Do with Their Money*, remarks, "The more you can have open and honest communication with yourself and with your family, the better off you'll be. A lot of the problems that arise in personal finance have nothing to do with math. They have nothing to do with looking at the numbers. They have to do with your emotions. One of the biggest struggles people have is overcoming their emotional attachment to money, good and bad. If we can talk about money a little bit more and be honest with ourselves, that's the key. It's not hard to understand basic addition and subtraction, which is what most of personal finance is based on. What is hard is managing the emotions that prevent us from doing the things we should be doing for our own benefit and for our family's benefit. If you can understand that the key is more about your emotions than anything else, you'll be ahead of the game."

It's critical that we normalize discussions around money. Jim Cramer learned invaluable financial lessons from his father. In a *Mad Money* segment, he remarked, "People always ask me about how I know so much about money. I have to say, some of the best lessons I learned about money were from my father." In 1979, all of Cramer's possessions were stolen while he was living in Los Angeles, so he was forced to live in his car. He didn't have enough money to make a phone call. Cramer reached out to his father for guidance. His father told him he needed to obtain money to invest. After Cramer reiterated that he was living in his car, his father insisted, telling him, "The secret is to invest ten dollars at a time." Cramer managed to scrape together ten dollars every other week, and he invested that money in mutual funds. He declared that it paid off in the long run, admitting, "Pop, you were right."[15]

Personally, I have also been fortunate enough to have parents who involved me in financial decisions from a young age. Sometimes it was as simple as, "Do you think it is a better choice to eat out for lunch or make a meal at home?" or "Should we take a taxi or walk?" Other times, my parents

---

15   Jim Pavia, "Mad Money's Jim Cramer Recalls 'Money Talks' with His Dad," *CNBC*, June 13, 2019.

involved me in decisions that were of more significance, such as deciding whether to lease or buy a car.

Gen Z has already overcome boundaries set by previous generations as they pertain to other taboo subjects, like politics and personal identity. We *can* do the same with money and ignite and lead conversations. The first step to being forthright about money is becoming educated and aware.

IDENTIFY YOUR PSYCHOLOGICAL HURDLES WITH MONEY

"People say don't be emotional about money. Everyone's emotional about money. It's a human reaction," says JJ Kinahan, chief market strategist at TD Ameritrade. It's okay to have emotions associated with money, but it's important that you don't allow your emotions to lead you to form psychological hurdles that will inhibit your financial success. Some common psychological hurdles related to money management are:

- I'm not good at math.
- I'm busy and don't have enough time.
- I'm young, so I have plenty of time before I need to begin.
- I don't have enough money.
- Personal finance and investing are complicated.

Throughout this book, I will try to arm you with the knowledge needed to overcome these psychological hurdles. The first step is to recognize that they are merely myths and mental obstacles that you have the power to conquer. It will take some diligence and effort, but it will be worth it. Let's take inspiration from Nike's motto and "Just do it."

START SMALL

This book will provide you with the information and tools you need to be financially successful. However, to derive the most benefit from it, you must take action and apply the principles presented. Louis Barajas, one of the first Latino CFP®s, observes, "Knowledge applied is power."

Many people who aim to lose weight spend days researching and composing the perfect diet, but then never actually follow their meal plan. They would likely reach their goals more quickly by implementing small and sustainable changes as opposed to attempting to completely revamp their entire lifestyle at once and then just giving up altogether. Small, consistent changes morph into big results. Choosing to make a change is the foundation of success. After taking that initial step, it becomes significantly easier to form habits that will eventually become second nature. The same is true of personal finance. It does not matter how much you read or how well-thought-out your financial plan is if you do not act. It is normal to be frightened of making a mistake. Most people do make slipups, but the key is to learn from those missteps. Figure out what went wrong and think about how you can improve next time. View the missteps as opportunities for growth. The consequences of making financial mistakes early in life are less significant than making the same blunders later in adulthood when the stakes are much greater.

I get it. Learning about money can be intimidating, but starting small can help immensely. Think of learning about money in the same way that you would think about learning a new language. When learning a new language, you begin with the basics, such as "hello," "goodbye," "thank you," "yes," and "please." Over time, you gain fluency and become more comfortable speaking the language. The more you immerse yourself in the language and surrounding culture, the more proficient you become. The same goes for money. Start by devoting ten to fifteen minutes per day to learning about personal finance and investing. You will be amazed at how quickly your knowledge (and hopefully your profits) compound.

TALK TO YOUR FRIENDS

Chances are, your friends share many of your financial concerns, whether it is paying for college or getting a job. You can learn from each other and create your own financial community. Actively engage in discussions about savings tips and different approaches to investing. You can learn so much from and greatly expand your horizons with these conversations.

Tiffany "the Budgetnista" Aliche has three components she believes are the foundation of financial success. She explains, "Knowledge, access, and community. You have to seek knowledge. Take a class, ask questions; you're going to have to learn from other people. Then, access—access comes from other people. There's only so much you can learn watching a YouTube channel, or reading a book. You should actually connect with people who have accomplished some of the same financial goals you've accomplished. Personally, I have a financial planner even though I do my own finances. I recognize it is important to have people who are smarter than me in my circle to take me to the next level. Last, community—community is a critical component in transforming and taking yourself to the next level because it provides accountability and normalization of the process. If you follow these three principles, you are well on your way to success in this space."

SET GOALS

"I encourage people to set goals because having something specific you are trying to achieve will help you manage your money better," says Tim Sheehan, founder and CEO of Greenlight.

CFP® and former NFL player Jedidiah Collins remarks, "If you want to be successful, you have to begin with a definite purpose. I'm not saying your goal is one million dollars . . . that's not a goal; that's a number. Your goal is what you truly want. What does that one million dollars reflect? Do you want to live in the Bahamas? Do you want to drive a fancy car or own a nice house? Do you want to support your parents? Do you want to support a cause? What are you going to do with that one million dollars?"

Begin by figuring out your "why." What does success mean or look like for you? What can money do for you? Visualize where you want to be in the future and set goals that align with your values. It's important to not just think about *what* you want to do but also *why* you want to do it. Then, write down three financial goals: one short-term goal you wish to achieve within the next year, one medium-term goal you wish to achieve within the next three to five years, and one long-term goal that will take more than five years to achieve. Keep in mind that long-term goals may be built upon short-term goals.

***

Barajas said it best when he told me, "Wealth begins in the mind." Money can generate a lot of emotions like jealousy and resentment, but it can also bring a feeling of empowerment and accomplishment. It's up to you.

Z NOTES

- Identify your personal psychological hurdles with money and begin to work on overcoming them. You can do this!
- Devote a few minutes per day to increasing your financial literacy. Your knowledge will compound over time.
- Set realistic short- and long-term goals that will help you stay the course on your financial journey.
- Create your own financial community.

CHAPTER 3

Saving Savvy

"Do not save what is left after spending, but spend what is left after saving."

—WARREN BUFFETT

Saving already plays a bigger role in your life than you realize. You are saving half of your Chipotle burrito bowl to eat later. You saved a souvenir from your spring break trip to Europe. However, saving goes beyond Mexican food and trinkets. Saving money is the foundation of a financially secure future.

EVERYDAY MILLIONAIRES

The Millionaire Next Door by William Danko and Thomas J. Stanley reveals many interesting insights. For one, it offers the revelation that a day in the life of a typical millionaire doesn't revolve around wearing a fur coat and shades, plunking ten shopping bags in a bright red Lamborghini, and then driving home to a summer mansion in Beverly Hills. In reality, many of the people living these lavish lifestyles are drowning in debt. Rather, many millionaires are inconspicuous and frugal. They view money as a tool and live below their means, spending much less than they can afford. They tend to drive older cars and do not eat out or shop very frequently, *saving* what they can.

THE BENEFITS OF SAVING

Most people save with similar intentions: to gain a sense of security and to reach their life goals. You may need to save to pay for your education, to purchase a car, to support your family, or to fund a semester abroad.

Saving enables you to benefit from compound interest. As you will learn, the more you are able to save, the more you can invest and allow your money to grow for your future self!

People also save to build their ***emergency fund***, a stash of money earmarked for unexpected expenses life throws your way. An emergency fund serves as a financial cushion and can keep you afloat in times of need without having to rely on credit cards or high-interest loans. Let's face it: the future is unknown, and you *will* have financial surprises in your life.

Take it from Sharon Epperson, CNBC's senior personal finance correspondent. September 21, 2016, began as an ordinary day for Epperson. After eating breakfast and sending her kids off to school, she attended an exercise class at the gym before work. During the class, Epperson felt an unusual, sharp pain in the back of her head and neck. Instead of trying to finish her workout, she asked her husband to pick her up; the pain was so severe, she didn't think it wise to drive.

Epperson's husband drove her to a doctor who had an emergency room background. Recognizing something was gravely wrong, the doctor immediately sent her to a local hospital where a CT scan revealed bleeding in Epperson's brain; she had suffered a ruptured brain aneurysm. About two-thirds of those who survive the condition suffer from a permanent neurological impairment. Luckily, Epperson survived, but she had to receive extensive recuperative therapy. She was unsure if she would ever be able to return to her job and old lifestyle again. Of course, the last thing on her mind was her finances. The brain aneurysm took Epperson completely by surprise, as she had no known risk factors. After the fact, Epperson was grateful she had an emergency fund and an organized system for her finances in place.[16]

Epperson's story epitomizes the vital importance of a financial cushion, as you never know what may happen in life. Tim Sheehan, founder and CEO of Greenlight, explains, "Say your car needs to be fixed. That's likely not an expense you have in your monthly budget because it's not an expense you have every month. That's where your savings come in. A lot of people don't have those savings set aside, so they end up having to pay for the car repairs with a credit card, which can lead them to build high-interest credit card debt. Your job is usually paying you enough money to cover your monthly bills. There's often very little money left over to pay off that debt. By having some savings set aside, you can pay for that car repair or unexpected expense without having to go into debt."

---

16   Laura Haverty, "Surviving a Brain Aneurysm Taught Me This About Personal Finance," *NBC News*, April 26, 2019.

"The pandemic left a lot of people in a financially precarious position," says Jennifer Barrett, chief education officer of Acorns. "I hope one of the lessons that comes from the pandemic is that we need to take our savings more seriously. We need to take advantage of the good times to save enough money to get us through the bad times."

A rule of thumb is to have enough money saved to cover three to six months of basic living expenses (needs like rent, utilities, and food) if you are responsible for all your own expenses. Building an emergency fund takes time, so set micro goals. Aim to save enough money to cover a few weeks of living expenses and work your way up from there. In the next chapter, we will talk about how to calculate your monthly expenses and how to optimize your money via a cash flow plan.

Plus, doesn't saving make you feel like you got something for free? It's exhilarating when you go to buy a pair of headphones and discover it is marked down. It's also a fabulous feeling when you check your bank account statement and see you have more saved than you thought. Saving is empowering.

SAVING WHEN YOU ARE STRAPPED FOR CASH

It can be easy to mentally scan your finances and feel overwhelmed at the prospect of saving money. You may feel that you are barely scraping by as is and cannot afford to save any extra dollars. Perhaps you earn minimum wage and are working a part-time job. In this chapter and the next, I will share tips with you on how to save small amounts of money that can add up over time, no matter your financial situation.

IT'S THE LITTLE THINGS

It's easy to make small purchases that don't seem like they are going to break your wallet without giving them a second thought. Whether or not to buy a $5 latte is likely not a tough decision. It doesn't feel like you're spending a significant sum of money. We tend to spend much more time deliberating over what we perceive as an expensive, one-time purchase, such as those $250 AirPods that everybody seems to be wearing. In reality, though, small purchases add up and can collectively be significantly more costly over the long run.

If you buy five $5 lattes every week, you are spending $1,300 on drinks per year (fifty-two weeks x $25). These $5 coffees represent virtually any of your frequent purchases, whether it's in-app purchases, smoothies, or boba. What if you saved that $1,300 instead? Of course, I am not saying to give up all the little things that bring you joy. However, consider that you would save $520 per year if you cut out two of those weekly lattes; perhaps you could buy a pair of AirPods after six months by cutting out a couple lattes every week. Perhaps the savings accumulated from going on a latte cleanse for one year could buy you a computer. Maybe a few years' worth of coffee equates to a used car for you.

This concept is known as opportunity cost. Opportunity cost can be thought of as opportunity lost. The opportunity cost of watching TV instead of doing your homework is a good grade. In this context, opportunity cost refers to the reality that each financial decision you make involves multiple facets. When you regularly make small, mindless purchases instead of saving and investing, you could be losing out on an even greater potential gain down the road.

Little drops of rain form a large ocean. Author David Bach popularized this notion as "the latte factor." This term represents the small, unconscious purchases that we make each day. It is based on the concept that saving and/or investing the aggregate of these small purchases is powerful. Saving and building wealth is not necessarily about how much income you generate—it oftentimes boils down to your spending habits.

$5 coffee
2 x /week=$520 / year

AirPods

I encourage you to think about some of the small, frequent purchases that you might be willing to cut back on or give up altogether in order to progress toward your goals. It's not about being cheap; it's about prioritizing what you value. Could you get tap water instead of soft drinks when you dine at restaurants? Doing so could save you $1 to $3 each time you eat out. Could you pack your own lunch? A $10 lunch at Chick-fil-A four times per week adds up to $2,080 per year! Do the math on your frivolous purchases. Whatever you spend your money on, it's critical that you are aware that small purchases add up over time—each dollar you save brings you one step closer to achieving your financial goals! Of course, you should still enjoy little treats. Just be mindful of your cash flow. The more you put delayed gratification into practice, the more natural it will become.

There are many services nowadays that can help you save. Bank of America's Keep the Change® Savings Program automatically rounds up the purchases you make with the bank's debit card to the nearest dollar. For example, if you purchase a salad for $9.70, the service rounds up your purchase to $10 and transfers the extra $0.30 out of your checking account and into your savings account. Qapital is a mobile platform that allows you to set rules to automate your savings. For instance, each time you spend money from a linked funding account, Qapital can round up your purchase to the nearest dollar and move the difference into a goal account.

If you have the psychological hurdle of "I don't have enough money," I hope you begin to view your expenditures with a bit more of a critical eye. No amount is too small to save. As

I said in the last chapter, small changes and actions beget big results.

SET YOURSELF UP FOR SUCCESS: THE POWER OF AUTOMATION

As humans, we often make decisions based on emotion rather than reason. For instance, attending a party if you have a major test the next day you haven't studied for would be an example of making a decision rooted in emotion rather than logic. This concept also applies to personal finance.

CFP® Carl Richards coins it "The Behavior Gap." After Richards studied the long-term returns of the overall stock market and compared them with the returns of individual investors, he discovered that the investors consistently underperformed in the overall market. He explains the difference, the behavior gap, as humans' tendency to allow emotions to influence our decisions. For example, this could manifest as buying a particular stock based on what friends are doing without researching it first.

Emotions are powerful, but they can lead you to make imprudent financial decisions, such as making a big purchase that you can't yet afford or blowing all your savings on an extravagant vacation with friends because of fear of missing out (FOMO).

The solution to this is to create systems. Louis Barajas, one of the first Latino CFP®s, explained to me, "I get people wealthy in the barrio by automating everything. How? Well, as soon as they start working and get out of college, I fill out the paperwork so they can start their 401(k) plan. I open a brokerage account for them, and we have money coming out of their checking account every month. If they have credit cards, we ensure they are paying the minimum due so if they forget to make a payment, their credit stays good. To me, it's building habits by creating systems around those habits. Left to our own accord, we don't always have the willpower."

Consider the things you do every day without thinking about it. For example, you most likely brush your teeth each morning without much thought. Now, think about habits which you are having trouble adopting. Perhaps these are studying daily or eliminating stress snacking. The corresponding bad habits inhibiting success have likely become automatic. Many successful people did not start out with all good habits; they have been able to transform bad habits into good ones and make the good habits automatic by creating systems. For example, someone who exercises each morning may lay out their workout clothes and sneakers the night before and place their alarm across the room so they are forced to get up. For them, getting out of bed to hit the gym is no longer difficult.[17]

Luckily, it has never been easier to automate and create systems for your finances. A great area of your finances to automate is your savings. In doing so, you take emotions, impulses, and thinking out of the equation.

By sending your dollars to a bank account before you have the opportunity to spend them, you won't spend them. They

---

17   David Weliver, "Put Your Money on Autopilot," *Money Under 30*, April 17, 2019.

are out of sight, out of mind. Jennifer Barrett, chief education officer of Acorns, says, "Automating your good habits is one of the smartest things you can do. When you get in the habit of doing something, there's an inertia force that keeps you from wanting to change it, which works in your favor with automation."

Kelly DiGonzini, director of financial planning at Beacon Pointe, agrees. She recommends, "Get in the habit of saving, even if it's ten dollars or twenty dollars per week. Then when you get your first job, maybe start saving one hundred dollars per week, but just get in the habit of saving—not spending—everything you have. Set up a recurring automatic transfer—whether it's every week, twice a month, or once a month—into a savings account you don't look at regularly. Then, in small increments, increase the dollar amount over time. Alternatively, you could even automatically save a percentage of your income. That way, the aggregate amount of money saved increases as your income does."

DiGonzini went on to describe how, contrary to popular belief, your discretionary wealth is typically the highest when you first begin working because, although you are likely generating the least income you ever will, you probably also have the fewest financial responsibilities with no children or mortgage. This is the time when you should be saving the largest percentage of your income.

Lauryn Williams, four-time Olympian and CFP®, recommends, "Pay yourself first. Oftentimes, all these people line up, and you're trying to be responsible, and you realize, 'Oh, I've gotta pay the landlord! I have to pay the light bill. I have to pay so-and-so.' I kind of just imagine all these people lined up with their hands out. But you need to put yourself at the front of that line and put your own hand out first. For every paycheck you earn, make sure you put a portion of it away for yourself. I usually recommend 20 percent, but it depends on what you are trying to accomplish. Generally, though, about 20 percent of whatever you earn should be going back into your own pocket for various goals, whether that's building your emergency fund, saving for retirement, or funding a down payment on your first home. If you earn one hundred dollars, put twenty bucks away. Then say, 'Okay, I have eighty dollars left. Who else needs to be paid?' That way, you set up your other expenses in a way that allows you to live within your means."

Systematically saving ensures that you don't fall victim to your excuses. Putting your money on autopilot is perfect for you if you have the financial psychological hurdle of "I'm busy and don't have enough time." The best part about automating your savings is that you can set it and forget it. Establishing an automatic savings plan is the best way to pay yourself first, and it only involves two simple steps.

1. Establish Two Separate Bank Accounts

There are multiple different types of bank accounts, which we will discuss in depth in another chapter. For the sake of putting your savings on autopilot, you only need to be familiar with two types: checking accounts and savings accounts. Funds in a checking account are typically used for daily purchases, such as gas and groceries. Meanwhile, a savings account is just what it sounds like—it's an account in which you save money. As you are saving money in the account, you do not frequently withdraw from it. You can nickname your bank accounts, so be creative!

2. Set Up an Automatic Transfer

Most banks allow you to arrange recurring transfers from one bank account to another via their online platform or mobile app. Simply select the account that you want to transfer "from" and the account that you want to transfer "to." Enter the dollar amount that you would like to transfer, as well as how frequently you would like the transfer to occur. For example, each week.

This is how it works: Kelly has asked her bank to automatically transfer $50 from her checking account to her savings account biweekly. She deposits the $250 she earns through babysitting and her part-time job into the checking account. The bank automatically transfers $50 to her savings account every two weeks. Voila! Kelly has $50 stashed in her savings account and $200 in her checking account. She can spend the money in her checking account, or she can route it to other accounts, such as her investment account.

When it comes to putting money on autopilot, Gen Z has an advantage. Even just a decade ago, direct deposits were groundbreaking. Today, with the advent of new and improved technologies, it is easier than ever to automate saving. Humphrey Yang, a former financial advisor who runs a personal finance TikTok with nearly two million followers, comments, "I love automating if possible, especially when it comes to your paycheck. If you can set aside certain parts of your paycheck to different accounts—even better."

***

Jennifer Barrett, chief education officer of Acorns, says, "If everyone got in the habit of living on 80 percent of their income and saving and investing the rest, people would have enough saved for retirement and enough saved to get them through tough times. That's one of the things I would really like to see change with this new generation . . . living on 80 percent of their income and saving and investing the rest could make a huge difference for Gen Z."

Saving money is power. It not only affords you the freedom to buy the items of your dreams, but it also (more importantly) gives you a feeling of security and wellbeing in knowing that you will be able to financially weather whatever life throws your way. An emergency fund is like an insurance policy that allows you to sleep soundly at night. Saving also sets you up to harness the amazing power of compound growth, which we will discuss in another chapter. Saving money is not always the easy choice, but as Zoomers, we like to walk the path less taken!

FUN FACTS
- The most common reason Americans tap their emergency funds is for major home repairs, followed by car expenses.[18]
- In April 2020, during the COVID-19 pandemic, the personal savings rate in the United States hit a record 33 percent.

---

18   Joel Anderson, "Survey Finds Most Common Reasons Americans Use Emergency Funds," *GoBankingRates*, May 24, 2018.

Z NOTES:

- People save to reach their goals, to establish an emergency fund, and to take advantage of compound growth.
- An emergency fund is a stash of money earmarked for unexpected expenses and should cover three to six months of basic living expenses (whatever this looks like for you).
- Automation allows you to prioritize saving and prevents you from falling victim to your excuses. To establish an automatic savings plan, set up two bank accounts and establish a recurring transfer between them.
- Little expenses add up. Each time you make a purchase, consider the opportunity cost.

CHAPTER 4

Managing Your Cash Flow

———

"It's clearly a budget. It's got a lot of numbers in it."
—*GEORGE W. BUSH*

When CFP® and former NFL player Jedidiah Collins received his first big paycheck as a rookie, he spent every dime of it. Many professional athletes spend extravagantly and eventually find themselves broke and living paycheck to paycheck (like the majority of Americans). The prospect of having a similar relationship with money frightened Collins. The night after he spent the paycheck, he awoke "in knots and sweat." This experience awakened Collins to the reality that he needed to have a plan for his finances and for his spending to make his money work for him.

WHY HAVING A PLAN FOR YOUR MONEY IS IMPORTANT

Your finances were most likely simple when you were twelve or thirteen. Maybe you earned an allowance and occasionally treated yourself to a Frappuccino or a new book. As you've gotten older, though, your finances have likely gotten a bit more complicated just like the rest of your life. With more freedom comes more choices and concomitant opportunities to spend your money. You may be going out with your friends more often and to more expensive places than when you were young. Your obligations have also increased. Perhaps you are beginning to think about financing college or purchasing a car. If you are in college, you may have to worry about rent, utilities, and groceries. You begin to understand the harsh reality that your needs have expanded and that you have limited means.

The freedom that comes with getting older is exciting, but it also comes with increased financial responsibility, which can be overwhelming. Before the end of each month, many individuals find themselves out of money. Unsure of exactly where their dollars went, they are uncertain about how to move forward and improve the next month. This is why having an effective tool to show you where your money goes is central to achieving financial success. Luckily, a cash flow plan can help you. You may know this tool better by the term "budget." "Budget" has a negative connotation because many people associate it with restriction and penny pinching. Nevertheless, a plan for your money is an invaluable tool in reaching your financial goals.

Fundamentally, a cash flow plan is a tool to keep track of what is going out (expenses) versus what is coming in (income).

Not knowing where your money is going makes it difficult to progress toward your financial goals. A cash flow plan enables you to gain awareness about your spending habits and allows you to spend in alignment with your values and priorities. The downward spiral of debt begins when you spend more than you have. As implied by the name, a cash flow plan helps you plan. Creating a plan for tackling your expenses can prevent you from spending more than you can afford and carrying a credit card balance. Collins advises, "Employ your money. Make sure all your dollars are going to work for you."

Keep in mind that you may only need to create a cash flow plan every few months or years as long as you are living within your means and are aware of where your money is going. Okay, enough talk. Here's how to actually create one:

1. **Decide how long you would like to track your expenses for.** This can be one week, two weeks, or one month—whatever you feel will give you an accurate picture of your spending.
2. **Calculate your post-tax income.** Add up the amount of money you earn from all your different income streams, including jobs and side hustles. Make sure that your income aligns with the length of time you are tracking your expenses (i.e., if you track your expenses for a month, calculate your monthly after-tax income).
3. **Create a spending journal.** Come up with a method for tracking your expenses. You may choose to create a list on your phone, which is a great choice because chances are you have it with you most places you go. Alternatively, you could create an Excel or Google spreadsheet.

A plethora of budgeting apps are also available which generate snazzy pie charts and graphics of your spending. These tools make it easy to identify and analyze patterns in your spending. Track the items you purchase by date and keep track of recurring expenditures (such as monthly bill payments).

- Bills
- Car
  - Auto insurance
  - Gas
  - Maintenance
- Charity
- Clothing and Shoes
- Entertainment
  - Books
  - Concerts
  - Movies
  - Video games
- Food
  - Eating Out
  - Groceries
- Gym
- Gifts
- Hobbies
- Home Maintenance/Repair
- Insurance
- Internet Service
- Laundry
- Personal Hygiene (such as haircuts)
- Phone
- Public Transportation (Ubers, train)

- Rent/mortgage
- Retirement and Investment Contributions
- Saving
- Subscriptions (music, streaming services, news)
- Travel
- Tuition

4. **Subtract your expenses from your income.** A positive number indicates you are living below your means; you can give the extra dollars you have a job. A negative number indicates you need to carefully evaluate where your money is going—the next step is especially important for you.

5. **Analyze.** A spending journal allows you to become cognizant of patterns in your spending. Assign categories to each of your expenses, as doing so allows you to see which types of expenses are taking the biggest bite out of your income. If you discover something you weren't aware of, readjust your habits to better align with your goals. It may take a bit of prioritization; ask yourself what's important to you. Do you really need that new pair of jeans or can you reallocate that money toward your savings?

6. **Calculate your discretionary income.** Go back through your expenses, and this time, only subtract your basic living expenses from your total income. The remainder is your discretionary income. You can choose what to do with your discretionary income, but be sure to allocate a significant portion of it toward saving, investing, and other goals.

7. **Set spending limits for each category.** For instance, cap your entertainment spending at $150 per month. Limits guide your spending.

THE 50/30/20 RULE

Deciding how to balance your income with your various expenses is important. Consider a 50/30/20 allocation. This method is simple and offers a structure to guide your spending while affording you flexibility. It involves dividing your post-tax income into three categories: needs, wants, and goals.

	Percentage	Examples
Needs	50	Rent, groceries, utilities
Wants	30	Entertainment, shopping, travel
Goals	20	Saving, investing, funding a down payment on a home

CONTROLLING YOUR SPENDING

"Beware of little expenses. A small leak will sink a great ship."

—BENJAMIN FRANKLIN

Spending money is easy. Making *wise* spending decisions that align with your goals is more challenging, but it is certainly possible and becomes easier with time. Let's take a look at a few tips and tales for inspiration.

LIVE LIKE A BILLIONAIRE

If you are trying to manage your cash flow and develop smart spending habits, you may want to try living like a billionaire, but only if that billionaire is Warren Buffett. A famous investor and the CEO of Berkshire Hathaway,

Buffett is often dubbed the "Oracle of Omaha." However, despite his roughly $74 billion net worth, he enjoys a simple life.

Buffett has said, "I buy everything I want in life. Would ten homes make me [happier]? Possessions possess you at a point. I don't like a $100 meal as well as a hamburger from McDonald's." Many people associate billionaires with sprawling mansions and opulent possessions. However, Buffett lives in the same Omaha residence he purchased in 1958 for $31,500, which is the equivalent of roughly $270,000 in 2017 dollars. He claims he eats McDonald's for breakfast every day, spending no more than $3.17 each time. Additionally, he used a $20 flip phone for years until he finally upgraded to an iPhone 11 in 2020. Buffett's frugality also extends to his automobile preferences. In 2014, he purchased a new Cadillac XTS-luxury sedan after his daughter, Susie, convinced him his 2006 Cadillac DTS was too embarrassing. He auctioned off the old Cadillac to a bidder who paid $122,500; Buffett donated this money to a charity called Girls Inc. of Omaha.[19]

With that said, Buffett has had some luxurious possessions over the years. He once said his private jet was a luxury because it saves him so much time. Additionally, he once had a beachfront property in Laguna Beach, California, which he sold for $7.5 million in 2018.[20] However, all things considered, Buffett lives significantly below his means.

---

19 Jodi O'Connell, "5 of Warren Buffett's Most Frugal Habits," *Business Insider*, May 21, 2017.

20 Tom Huddleston Jr., "How Warren Buffett Spends His Billions," *CNBC*, August 19, 2020.

LIVING IN A TRUCK

After Brandon graduated college, he accepted a job offer from Google; he had previously interned for the company. During his internship experience, he learned he really didn't need an apartment. For the three months he interned, he lived in a "super expensive" apartment he shared with several other people. Every day, he would catch the first bus in the morning, work out at his office, get breakfast there, work, eat lunch with his team, do a bit more work, have dinner at the office, then hang out with friends. As he wasn't spending much time at his apartment, he resolved he would try to live in a truck if he got a full-time job at Google. As Brandon puts it, "I figured the only thing I really needed was a bed . . . I didn't need the whole apartment thing. That kind of forced me to live minimally and forced me out into the world. It was a very useful savings vehicle."

As soon as Brandon began his job at Google, he bought a truck. Eventually, he began blogging and sharing his experiences. "I learned just how little I actually needed. I had to figure out what to do with the extra money I had from not having to pay rent. I learned about investing. From my perspective, the goal has always been flexibility. Money is not the end itself; it's a means to an end. For me, I think that end is financial independence. Living in the truck has allowed me to save more money than I otherwise could have. I noticed when you buy things, you tend to buy even more things. However, the opposite is also true. When you recognize where the consumption is in your life, you actively seek to cut that out . . . it has a sort of multiplying snowball effect." Brandon says learning this lesson early on gave him the resources he needed to invest and work toward financial independence earlier.

Although you do not need to live in a truck like Brandon to achieve financial independence, you should take two things away from his story:

- Think about how you can cut back on your expenses.
- Find creative ways to save.

DISCOUNTS

In 1887—one year after Coke was introduced—Coca-Cola created the first ever coupon. These coupons could be redeemed for one free glass of Coke at any dispensary. This marketing strategy greatly benefitted Coca-Cola and turned it into a household name. Americans redeemed their coupons at local pharmacies and kept coming back for more. Pharmacy owners turned to Coca-Cola to replenish their Coke supply as demand grew.[21] Since then, hundreds of thousands of companies have taken inspiration from Coca-Cola and adopted promotions and coupons.

As a consumer, you can greatly benefit from discounts if you are already planning to purchase an item. However, if you are *not* planning to purchase something, they can lead to unnecessary spending. If you see the original price of an item

---

21   Danny Wong, "What Science Says About Discounts, Promotions and Free Offers," *Huffington Post*, November 10, 2015.

and then its sales price, you are comparing the sales price to the original price. Therefore, it is only natural to feel the sales price is a steal. Purchasing something marked down from $75 to $45 feels fantastic. However, in reality you must ask yourself whether you need—or even want—the $45 item. Are you buying it simply because it is on sale and seems like a bargain? Don't buy something just for the sake of buying it; be deliberate with your spending. Money spent is money spent, whether it's $10 or $200.

THE COUPON KID

In 2016, Gen Zer and United Kingdom resident Jordon Cox wanted to get home to Brentwood, outside London, from Sheffield. He chose to take the cheapest possible route: he flew via Berlin, Germany. By flying in lieu of taking the train, Cox saved around eleven US dollars. In Britain, many know him as "the coupon kid" because of the reputation he has built as a saving and couponing master. After Cox's parents separated, he and his mother didn't have the financial security that they previously did; his father was the primary breadwinner. Cox was inspired to begin seeking ways to save small sums of money after watching *Extreme Couponing* (an American show). After Cox helped his mother save a bit on groceries the week after his father left, he was hooked.[22] These days, couponing has never been easier because of mobile apps such as Ibotta, SnipSnap, and ShopSavvy.

---

22   Jodie Smith, "Money-Saving Teen Jordon Cox: From Blogging to Berlin," *BBC News*, February 6, 2016.

MY TWO CENTS

When buying an article of clothing or piece of jewelry, I focus on the cost per wear. If you have a sixty-dollar pair of jeans and wear it twice, the cost per wear is thirty dollars. If you wear that pair of jeans sixty times, the cost per wear is one dollar. One year, I bought a plush, dark gray hoodie from Athleta that I absolutely loved. Because I am someone who is cold when it is seventy degrees outside, I have worn that hoodie practically every fall and winter day. I wear it to the grocery store and to school; it is a staple. The cost per wear for this hoodie is likely fractional. Be thoughtful and intentional in your purchases.

BE CAUTIOUS OF WHAT YOU CAN'T SEE

Chris Brown, the manager of fintech startup WalletFi, advises, "Manage your spending as if you actually had a piggy bank or stash you had to empty out every time you made a purchase. Many companies these days like Netflix, Hulu, and Xbox have a subscription purchase model. It's all just an automatic five bucks or twenty bucks out of your account. It's easy to sign up for services that are all relatively inexpensive on their own. A decent chunk of your income is already gone before you receive your paycheck or allowance as it's already promised to these services. It's essentially unconscious spending. To be really on top of where your money is going, cancel services you don't use anymore, and make sure you know when free trials are about to convert to something." Apps like Trim and TrueBill analyze your spending to help you manage subscriptions and negotiate various bills.

***

Think of yourself as a business. All businesses spend and earn, just like you. However, a good business spends less than it earns to be profitable. Furthermore, *great* businesses reinvest their profits in themselves for future growth.

With what I call the "Tech Revolution," there have never been more digital tools available to help you achieve financial success. These include budgeting apps like Mint and You Need a Budget (YNAB). Browser extensions like Honey and websites like RetailMeNot can also help you find great deals.

Each person has a unique approach to spending and budgeting. Each person has also had different life experiences that have affected how they feel about money and, subsequently, how they spend it. Understand your deep-rooted feelings about money and then work to take the emotion out of your spending habits. Choose the tools that work best for you, and most importantly, live within your means no matter how much your heart is telling you to buy that new tablet or Tesla! Ultimately, it all comes down to dollars and cents.

FUN FACTS
- Your spending may shift as your lifestyle does. During COVID-19 lockdowns, Americans spent about 6 percent more on health and fitness and around 23 percent less on entertainment.[23]
- Consumer spending accounts for 70 percent of US GDP.

---

23 Megan Leonhardt, "64% of Americans Changed Their Spending Habits During the Pandemic—Here's How." *CNBC*, September 29, 2020.

Z NOTES

- A budget is a financial plan that guides you on how much to spend and on what.
- A budget can help you ensure you are living within your means (not spending more than you earn).
- View your money as a valuable tool to help you achieve your goals; you cannot make it work for you if you don't know where it is going.
- Apps can help you keep track of your spending and see where your money is going.

CHAPTER 5

Adulting: Taxes

"Taxes are the price we pay for a civilized society."
—US SUPREME COURT JUSTICE OLIVER WENDELL HOLMES

In 1930, Mahatma Gandhi decided he had had enough. India had fallen under British rule, and the British had implemented laws that made it illicit for Indians to gather or sell salt, which was a staple in their diet. Indians were forced to purchase the mineral from a British monopoly, which charged a hefty tax. In protest, Gandhi engaged in an act of peaceful civil disobedience by trekking over two hundred forty miles to Dandi, a village on the coast of the Arabian Sea, to collect salt. Thousands of frustrated Indians joined him along the way. When Gandhi reached his destination, he knelt down and picked up a small lump of salt from the ground, effectively transgressing the British law. The Salt March received considerable international coverage, prompting widespread indignation and drawing attention to the injustices Indians faced. As a result, Gandhi became the face of India's struggle for independence and the British began to view him as a force to be reckoned with.

Another example of the interesting role taxes have played in shaping our world is their contribution to a hostile relationship between the British and colonists in eighteenth century America. In 1764, the British Parliament enacted the Sugar Act, which imposed a tax on molasses. Then, it passed the Stamp Act in 1765, which taxed colonists for legal documents. As they felt that it was unfair for the British Parliament to levy taxes on the colonies without their say, the impassioned colonists cried, "No taxation without representation!" Finally, in 1767, the British government pushed the colonists over the edge after it passed legislation, called the Townshend Acts, that placed fresh taxes on items like tea and paint. Taxes were included in the list of grievances against King George III in the Declaration of Independence. Of course, opposition to the taxes, along with a host of other factors that contributed to the tension between the colonists and the British, culminated in the Boston Tea Party, a large war, and an independent America.[24]

THE TAXMAN

In 2018, the federal government received $3.33 trillion in taxes from individuals and corporations. Taxes are paid at the federal, state, and local levels. Although you might find them (tax)ing on your wallet, taxes play an important role in our society, and paying them is considered a civic duty. But when you write a check to Uncle Sam, where is your tax money going?

---

24 "Independence Day: Taxes Then and Now," Tax Foundation.

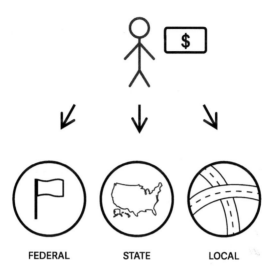

FEDERAL   STATE   LOCAL

Taxes fund government activities and expenditures. They ensure the machine that is the government remains well-oiled. More specifically, your hard-earned dollars contribute to infrastructure, national defense, public safety (firefighters and police officers), food stamps, and programs such as Medicare. Taxes also fund public education. If you attend or have attended a public high school, you may or may not have realized that the chairs, the textbooks, and the salaries of the teachers are all financed by taxes.

Governments may also levy taxes to try to influence the behavior of their citizens. Numerous governments have adopted carbon taxes—fees levied on the burning of carbon-based fuels. Carbon taxes are intended as a disincentive to the use of fossil fuels and to drive a shift toward clean energy.[25] Some governments also charge sin taxes. Sin taxes are taxes imposed on products and practices considered

---

25   "What's a Carbon Tax?" Carbon Tax Center.

detrimental, such as cigarettes and gambling, and are meant to discourage unhealthy behaviors.

In some places, a luxury tax (yes, that's the diamond ring space on the Monopoly board) is charged on items that are considered only affordable for very affluent consumers. In 1991, the government enacted a "yacht tax" in an effort to reduce the federal deficit. It included various luxury goods like furs, private jets, and (as the name suggests) yachts. In 1993, the tax was eliminated because some people argued that it was damaging the yacht industry. Governments may institute luxury taxes during wartime to increase federal revenue or to fund another large expense without raising taxes on the general population. As they only impact a small subset of the general population, most people are indifferent to and unaffected by luxury taxes.[26]

"In this world, nothing can be said to be certain, except death and taxes."

—BENJAMIN FRANKLIN

Taxes take several forms. They are often divided into two categories: direct taxes and indirect taxes. Direct taxes are, as the name implies, directly paid to the government by

---

26   Julia Kagan, "Luxury Tax," *Investopedia*, updated July 19, 2020.

taxpayers. Indirect taxes are collected by intermediaries, and consumers pay them when they purchase goods and services.

Taxes are also designated as regressive and progressive. Regressive taxes are charged uniformly, meaning everyone is taxed at the same rate. As a result, they financially squeeze low-income earners more than they do high-income earners. Progressive taxes are the opposite of regressive taxes. With progressive taxes, as individuals generate more income, they may pay more in taxes. Vertical equity is the idea that people who earn differing levels of income should pay different amounts of taxes, while horizontal equity is the idea that people who earn the same income should pay the same amount of taxes.

SALES TAX

Sales tax is an indirect tax. Stores collect this tax from their customers. Sales tax is governed at the state level, although shoppers and diners in some large cities, such as Los Angeles and Chicago, must pay the city's sales tax in addition to the state's sales tax. There are five states that do not impose a state sales tax: Alaska, Delaware, Montana, New Hampshire, and Oregon.

Let's look at an example of how this type of tax works. You purchase a t-shirt you've been eyeing at Sam's Shirts that costs $20, but the total on your receipt reads $21.40. The extra $1.40 reflects the 7 percent sales tax on the t-shirt. As all consumers are charged the same sales tax rate regardless of how much money they make, Elon Musk would pay the same $1.40 tax on the t-shirt if he bought it. Due to the regressive nature of sales taxes, they are rarely levied on prescription drug purchases.

INCOME TAXES

In the United States, *federal income tax* is a progressive tax, meaning people who earn higher taxable incomes pay more in federal income taxes. You are placed in a tax bracket based on the amount of taxable income you generate in a year. As of this writing, there are seven tax brackets.

2020 Federal Income Tax Brackets[27]

Rate	Taxable Income Bracket	Tax Due
10%	$0 to $9,875	10% of taxable income
12%	$9,876 to $40,125	$987.50 plus 12% over the amount over $9,875
22%	$40,126 to $85,525	$4,617.50 plus 22% of the amount over $40,125
24%	$85,526 to $163,300	$14,605.50 plus 24% of the amount over $85,525
32%	$163,301 to $207,350	$33,271.50 plus 32% of the amount over $163,300
35%	$207,351 to $518,400	$47,367.50 plus 35% of the amount over $207,350
37%	$518,401 or more	$156,235 plus 37% of the amount over $518,400

A common misconception is that all your taxable income is taxed at the single rate associated with your tax bracket.

---

27 Tina Orem, "2020–2021 Tax Brackets and Federal Income Tax Rates," *Nerdwallet*, April, 12, 2021.

Rather, your taxable income is split into "buckets." Let's look at an example to understand this concept.

The National Association of Colleges and Employers calculated the average starting salary for a class of 2018 graduate was about $50,004.[28] Let's say Jeremy just graduated college and earns $50,000 of taxable income. His income places him in the 22 percent tax bracket. How much does he owe in federal income taxes? Well, Jeremy pays 10 percent on the first $9,875 and 12 percent on the chunk of income between $9,876 and $40,125. Then he pays 22 percent on the rest because some of his taxable income falls into the 22 percent tax bucket. The total bill is around $6,800, approximately 14 percent of his taxable income, even though he is in the 22 percent tax bracket. That 14 percent is called his *effective tax rate*. Keep in mind this scenario only accounts for federal income taxes; your state may also charge you an income tax. There are only a handful of states that do not impose an income tax.

Another type of income tax is FICA (Federal Insurance Contributions Act). FICA is a US payroll tax, which means it is automatically withheld from your paycheck. You can picture this as Uncle Sam shaving a few bucks off a stack of Benjamins before the wad of bills hits your hands. FICA taxes fund the Social Security and Medicare programs. During tax season, your employer issues you a form called a *W-2*, which states the income you earned and the taxes withheld from your paycheck. The information on your W-2 is important when preparing your tax return.

---

28 Abigail Johnson Hess, "College Grads Expect to Earn $60,000 in Their First Job—Here's How Much They Actually Make," *CNBC*, February 17, 2019.

What is a 1040?

American taxpayers use the tax form 1040 to file their annual income tax returns. They use the form to calculate their taxable income and the taxes they owe on the income. Taxpayers also use the form to indicate their filing status (single or married) and *dependents* (children).

When do I have to file taxes?

You have to file taxes each year by Tax Day, which is usually in mid-April. However, there are rare exceptions. For example, in 2020, Tax Day was postponed until July 15 due to the extraordinary circumstances caused by the COVID-19 pandemic.

What is the IRS?

The *Internal Revenue Service (IRS)* is the United States government agency responsible for the collection of taxes and the enforcement of tax laws.

Louis Barajas was one of the first Latino CFP®s in the United States. In 1971, his father lost two jobs. He described to me, "We were basically going to lose the apartment and move into a car to live." Determined to make ends meet, however, his father "took off." He bought a welding machine and started his own business doing wrought iron work. Barajas recounts, "I grew up in a very impoverished neighborhood called Boyle

Heights. Boyle Heights is in East Los Angeles. Back then (and probably to this day) it was the hub of the Mexican American [community]. When [my father] started his business, I helped him with a business license and filled out the paperwork because I spoke English. One day, the IRS came knocking at our door and asked if he had filed his taxes. He hadn't. He looked at me because I was a translator. He asked me, 'You know how to do that?' I said, 'No. But if there's a book, I'll figure it out.' I said that because my parents were so young. I was also raised by my grandmother, and I had an uncle who used to love books. What would happen is he would always buy two books, and I would read with him. The way I made it out of the barrio is because I learned if I didn't have any mentors, I could read it. I could find out the information in a book. So, I asked my dad if he could take me to a bookstore, and we bought a book on how to prepare tax returns. There was no internet [and] no computers, or at least we didn't have access to any. I did this tax return by hand at the age of thirteen. When I was fifteen, we got audited for those tax returns. I went with my dad to the audit. He was asked who had prepared the tax returns, and he told them I had. The lady looked at me and said, 'How old are you?' I said, 'I'm only fifteen.' Then, she said, 'All these returns are two years old. You would have been only thirteen.' I said, 'Yes, I did the tax returns.' At the end of that audit, nothing happened. They didn't change anything. The IRS agent probably let us go because she felt bad for us. But after that meeting, I realized how important it was for me to learn about taxes."

DEDUCTIONS

The US tax system is rooted in voluntary compliance—the assumption that taxpayers report all income. Tax evasion—deliberately underpaying taxes—is illegal. However, tax avoidance— legally reducing your tax liability through claiming tax credits and *deductions*—is not. Deductions lower your taxable income, decreasing the amount of taxes you have to pay.

Taxpayers must choose between taking the standard deduction and itemizing. All taxpayers may elect to take the standard deduction. In 2020, this amount was $12,400 (the IRS adjusts this sum each year because of inflation). If you earned $60,000 per year and claimed the standard deduction, you would pay taxes on $47,600 in 2020. Meanwhile, itemizing allows you to claim deductions specific to your personal circumstances, such as interest paid on student loans and charitable donations. The majority of taxpayers take the standard deduction. Itemizing is more complicated than taking the standard deduction but can save some people more money. When choosing between the standard deduction and the itemized deduction, it is best to choose whichever deduction is better for your bank account.

TAX RETURNS

Filing a tax return entails calculating whether you owe the government taxes beyond what you have already paid, or if you have paid too much and are owed a tax refund. This is generally how it works:

1. You pay taxes throughout the year via payroll.

2. Around ten to twelve weeks before Tax Day, you receive your tax forms.
3. By April 15 (Tax Day), you complete your return and submit it to the IRS.
4. The IRS processes your return and either sends you a refund or requests more money.

Nowadays, the majority of Americans e-file. Automated e-filing software guides you through the process and calculates your taxes for you. Alternatively, you can go the DIY route by completing your taxes all by yourself and submitting your tax forms digitally to the IRS. In all, e-filing makes the process of filing taxes convenient, straightforward, and (relatively) painless.

***

Although taxes are not the most exciting topic to learn about, understanding them can save you thousands of dollars. Taxes provide essential services and resources, and everyone pays them, whether through sales tax on what they purchase or income taxes on what they earn. Plus, understanding how taxes work may help you better understand the tax policies that presidential candidates outline during contentious debates.

FUN FACTS

- Texans don't have to pay sales tax on cowboy boots.
- The pink tax refers to products and services that cost more for women than their equivalents cost for men. In fact, the New York City Department of Consumer Affairs found women pay an average of 7 percent more than men for similar products.[29]

Z NOTES

- Individuals and corporations pay taxes at the local, state, and federal levels to fund government expenditures and public spending.
- US federal income taxes follow a "progressive" system, meaning high-income earners pay more than low-income earners. Other types of taxes, such as sales tax, follow a "regressive" system.
- FICA is a federal payroll tax (aka it is automatically withheld from your paycheck) that funds the Medicare and Social Security programs.
- Tax deductions lower your taxable income.
- E-filing is the process of filing your taxes online.

---

29 Anna Bessendorf, *From Cradle to Cane: The Cost of Being a Female Consumer* (New York City, New York: New York City Department of Consumer Affairs, 2015), 5.

CHAPTER 6

Insurance 101

———

"There are worse things in life than death. Have you ever spent an evening with an insurance salesman?"

—WOODY ALLEN

Car crashes, fires, a broken wrist—nobody has a crystal ball to predict the future, and let's face it: unexpected disasters strike in life. The problem is that these surprises can result in financial catastrophes. That's where insurance comes in. Insurance helps you manage your financial risk. Along with your emergency fund, it is a critical component of your financial safety net. It ensures that if something unexpected happens to you, it doesn't result in financial disaster.

Jedidiah Collins, CFP® and former NFL player, says, "There are so many journeys that are derailed by accidents and mishaps. If you have the proper insurance, you have a little bit more peace of mind. To me, that's what money is all about . . . giving you peace of mind."

UNDERSTANDING INSURANCE POLICIES

By this point, you may be wondering: How do insurance companies make any money if they give it away for free? This is an excellent question. To understand the answer, let's take a look at insurance companies' business models.

PREMIUMS

Insurance companies make calculated bets. Policyholders regularly pay their insurance company a *premium*. In exchange, the insurance company financially supports the policyholder if they incur financial loss. An insurance company profits by collecting more money than it has to fork out. Generally, the cost of a premium increases as the amount of money an insurance company potentially has to pay you increases. A young male with a record full of traffic infractions and fender benders likely has to pay a higher premium than a middle-aged woman who has no history of penalties or car accidents. Young people usually have to pay higher premiums for auto insurance because they are considered less experienced drivers and theoretically a higher risk. Premiums are based on statistical probabilities that represent how much risk you pose for the insurance company (aka how likely they are to have to dish out money on your behalf).

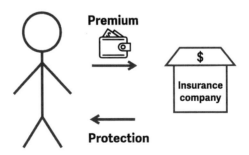

POLICY LIMIT

A policy limit is the maximum amount of financial coverage that an insurance company provides in a given policy. Insurance policies that include more than one type of insurance may have multiple coverage limits associated with the different types of insurance included in the policy.

DEDUCTIBLES

If you find yourself in a financial emergency, your insurance company will cover you, but only after you've paid your *deductible*. A deductible is a sum that you must pay out of pocket before insurance coverage kicks in. Deductibles range from a few hundred dollars to several thousand dollars. Your deductible depends on your policy. Let's say you get into a car accident and your vehicle needs $5,000 worth of repairs. Your plan has a $1,000 deductible. You would pay $1,000, and the insurance company would pay for the other $4,000 in repairs.

If your insurance policy has a per-claim deductible, you have to pay a deductible each time you file a separate claim. Some insurance policies (generally health insurance policies) have an annual deductible, meaning that you are covered by insurance once you meet your deductible for the year. Generally speaking, a plan with a low deductible corresponds with a higher premium and vice versa. Just like you, your insurer doesn't want to have to foot any huge bills.

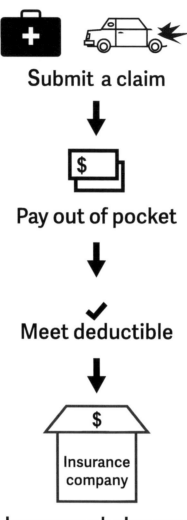

Submit a claim

Pay out of pocket

Meet deductible

$
Insurance
company

Insurance helps pay

COPAY

Most health insurance policies require that you shell out a copay each time you visit the doctor. A fixed amount, a copay is usually between twenty and thirty dollars. The copay is different from the deductible in an insurance policy, meaning that even if you meet your annual deductible, you may still have to pay a small fee at each medical appointment. If you meet your annual *out-of-pocket maximum,* which is a cap on the amount of money that you have to pay for healthcare expenses in a given year, you no longer have to worry about copays that year.

MAIN TYPES OF INSURANCE

There are many different types of insurance; each type protects people in different aspects of their lives. Your unique financial situation and obligations determine the specific policies you need to protect yourself and your loved ones. Note that some companies only sell one type of insurance, while others sell multiple types.

AUTO INSURANCE

Ah, it's the bane of many young adults' existence. Vehicle owners purchase auto insurance to mitigate the costs associated with getting into a car accident. Liability coverage covers the cost of medical bills and property damage for other drivers if you are at fault. Most US states mandate that all drivers have some liability insurance. Meanwhile, collision coverage covers the cost of damage to your own car. Comprehensive coverage covers damage to your car that does not necessarily result from a wreck, such as vandalism or a collision with a deer. The price of auto insurance depends on multiple factors, including your age, driving record, and gender.

HEALTH INSURANCE

Health insurance helps you remain financially stable if you fall ill or get hurt. This is how it works: You pay a monthly premium to a health insurance company, which, in turn, helps you cover your medical expenses. The majority of health insurance policies provide coverage for preventative visits, prescriptions, and other medical expenses. Several factors dictate how much you pay for health insurance. If you are young and healthy, you likely have to pay less for health insurance than a senior citizen who smokes and has multiple medical ailments.

A health insurance policy is a common employee benefit (the employer typically funds the premium). Medicaid currently provides health coverage to Americans with low incomes.

HOMEOWNERS AND RENTERS INSURANCE

Yup, there's a downside to moving out of your parents' house. In addition to paying your own bills, you have to purchase homeowners or renters insurance.

Homeowners insurance helps cover destruction to your home and possessions within your home. If a burglar broke in and stole $3,000 of your possessions, your homeowners insurance would help mitigate your losses.

Renters insurance is similar to homeowners insurance. A renters insurance policy covers personal belongings within a rented property. Your landlord is financially responsible for damage to the actual building. For example, if a fire destroyed all of the personal belongings you have within an apartment you rented, your personal property would only be covered through your renters insurance. Without this coverage, you would be responsible for the losses out of pocket. Luckily, renters insurance is quite affordable, costing an average of around fifteen dollars per month. For the cost of a meal out, it could save you hundreds of thousands of dollars.

UMBRELLA INSURANCE

Umbrella insurance provides supplemental liability coverage that goes beyond the limits of other policies. In other words, if your financial responsibility exceeds what other policies will help you pay, umbrella insurance coverage kicks in.

DISABILITY INSURANCE

Disability insurance is a type of insurance that provides you with financial support if you are medically unable to work. A means of covering basic living expenses, it provides you with a portion of the income you lose while unable to work. Disability insurance policies do not stipulate that you must pay a deductible before receiving a payout. There are two types of disability insurance: short-term disability insurance and long-term disability insurance. As the name implies, short-term disability insurance provides you coverage if an illness or injury leaves you unable to work for a short period of time. Meanwhile, long-term disability insurance covers the loss of income you might experience should you be deemed medically unable to work for an extended period of time.

LIFE INSURANCE

If you own a life insurance policy, an insurance company pays your *beneficiaries* if you pass away. A beneficiary may be a spouse or child.

There are two basic subcategories of life insurance: term life insurance and whole life insurance. Term life insurance provides life insurance coverage for a specific period of time. Meanwhile, whole life insurance remains in play for your entire life (not just a set time period) but costs significantly more.

***

It's just as, if not more, important to learn how to protect your money as it is to learn how to save and invest it. A solid understanding of insurance will serve you well on your financial journey. You work hard for your money, and the last thing you want is to lose any of it. Insurance helps you protect your wealth and maintain financial security in times of disaster.

FUN FACTS
- Cristiano Ronaldo's legs were insured for $144 million.
- Hayleigh Curtis—a Cadbury chocolate taster—has her taste buds insured for $1.33 million.[30]

---

30   Luke Graham, "10 Expensively Insured Body Parts," *CNBC*, September 9, 2016.

Z NOTES

- Insurance helps you protect your wealth and remain financially stable when disasters strike.
- When you purchase an insurance policy, you regularly pay an insurance company in exchange for some financial protection if something bad happens.
- Your unique financial situation and obligations determine the specific insurance policies you need to protect yourself and your loved ones. The main types of insurance are: health insurance, auto insurance, homeowners/renters insurance, life insurance, umbrella insurance, and disability insurance.

CHAPTER 7

Growing Your Own Money Tree: Compound Interest

———

"Compound interest is the eighth wonder of the world. He who understands it, earns it; he who doesn't, pays it."

—*ALBERT EINSTEIN*

"Would you be willing to lend me $10?" I remember asking my sister years ago.

"Okay. But you'll have to pay me back $11," she replied, grinning and rubbing her fingers together.

My experience is a perfect illustration of the cost of borrowing money. When someone lends you money, they do so with the expectation that they will end up with more. When my sister, who was acting like a bank, agreed to my request to borrow $10, she not only wanted the $10 back, but she wanted an additional $1. That additional $1 is called *interest*. Interest is the price of borrowing money. Lenders may charge you interest to profit and to mitigate the risk of not being repaid. Interest is a two-way street. If you are a borrower, you pay it. If you are a lender or an investor, you earn it. The amount of money you borrow or invest is the *principal*.

With that said, what is your relationship with a bank? Are you a borrower or a lender? Well, it depends. If you take out a loan, you become the borrower, and you have to pay interest. Meanwhile, if you deposit money, you become the lender, and you may receive interest. The interest a bank pays you over the course of a year is expressed as a rate. This rate is called the interest rate. If you keep $600 in a savings account at a bank and earn a 1 percent annual interest rate, you will have $606 after one year because the bank will have paid you $6 (1 percent x $600).

THE POWER OF COMPOUNDING

Would you rather receive a penny that doubles every day for a month or one million dollars? Let's find out. Imagine you have a single cent. Now, imagine it doubles every day. After two days, you have $0.02. After three days, you have $0.04. After a week, you have $0.64. After a month, or thirty days, you have $5,368,709 plus twelve cents.

A Penny Doubled Every Day for a Month

Day	Amount
1	$0.01
2	$0.02

3	$0.04
4	$0.08
5	$0.16
6	$0.32
7	$0.64
8	$1.28
9	$2.56
10	$5.12
11	$10.24
12	$20.48
13	$40.96
14	$81.92
15	$163.84
16	$327.68
17	$655.36
18	$1,310.72
19	$2,621.44
20	$5,242.88
21	$10,485.76
22	$20,971.52
23	$41,943.04
24	$83,886.08
25	$167,772.16
26	$335,544.32
27	$671,088.64
28	$1,342,177.28
29	$2,684,354.56
30	$5,368,709.12

That is the power of compounding. I imagine that you would opt for the doubling penny over the one million dollars.

Unfortunately, not everyone is lucky enough to receive a magic penny that doubles every day. Nevertheless, compounding is a powerful force to grow your money, so let's look at a different, more realistic example.

Imagine you receive a $500 graduation check from your grandmother. You have your eye on a new iPad but decide to invest the lump sum in the stock market to see what happens. You earn the market's average annual real 7 percent return.

Growing a $500 Lump Sum

Year	Beginning of the Year	End of the Year
1	$500	$535
2	$535	$572.45
3	$572.45	$612.52
4	$612.52	$655.40
5	$655.40	$701.28
20	$1,808	$1,935
30	$3,557	$3,806
50	$13,765	$14,729
100	$405,475	$433,858

Note: all figures are rounded after year five.

By the end of the first year, your $500 has grown to $535. You made thirty-five dollars. After the second year, your $535 grows to $572.45. You earned $37.45 By the end of the third year, your money has grown to $612.52. You made a little over forty dollars. Although you are earning the same 7 percent return, you are making a little more money each year. Your initial investment of $500 is growing, and your annual dollar return is growing. In less than eleven years, your money doubles. After forty-five years, your $500 has multiplied more than twenty-three times. Cha-ching!

What's going on? Well, your money is growing due to *compound interest*. During the first year, you earn a return on your $100 and make $7. During the second year, you earn a return on both your initial $100 and on the $7. The total amount you have at the end of one year becomes the amount on which you earn a return the next year. Compound interest is essentially interest earned on interest *and* the principal.

Let's compare compound interest to simple interest, or linear growth. While you earn interest both on the principal and on the interest that accumulates on it each period with compound interest, you only earn interest on the principal with simple interest. $500 growing linearly at a seven percent annual rate over five years earns $35 each year, totaling $675. Meanwhile, $500 compounding at a 7 percent annual rate leaves you with $709 after five years. This $34 difference may seem trivial to you. However, let's say you want to grow your $500 for fifty years. If you earn simple interest on your dollars, you will have $2,250 ($500 + fifty years x (.07 x 500)). Meanwhile, if your $500 compounds at a 7 percent annual rate for fifty years, you will be in possession of a whopping $16,390—a $14,140 difference. It adds up.

If the numbers from the $500 graduation check example don't yet excite you, let's see what happens when you regularly save and invest. Jenny is a twenty-year-old college student who decides to invest $100 every month for forty-five years until she plans to retire at age sixty-five. How much will she have when she turns sixty-five, assuming she earns a 7 percent annual return? $381,472. Wow—that's from saving the equivalent of $25 per week (five $5 coffees). Jenny invested a total of $54,000 and earned a return of $327,472. Through earning the stock market's average annual real return, Jenny ends up with six times the money she invested. Einstein was right. Compounding is one of the most powerful forces in the world.

Return: $327,472

Investment: $54,000

Sahil Bloom, an investor and financial education contributor, observes, "The concept of compounding applies broadly to life. Knowledge compounds in that you are building upon a base of what you already know. Relationships compound because you are building upon a base of trust. Learning about compound interest is powerful, and it encourages you to think long term about wealth creation and building your life and finances."

I encourage you to play with an online compound interest calculator to explore the power of compounding. Experiment with the rate of return, dollar amount invested, contributions, and years to grow. I like investor.gov and Acorns' compound interest calculators.

A GAME OF INCHES

"I was able to take away many lessons from the game of football and translate them into the world of finance. [There's] nothing more important than the idea of stealing inches. I got to work next to a fifteen-year veteran, a linebacker. Out on the field, (this is where I noticed it first) . . . [when] we would run forty yards, he ran forty-five. We'd run fifty, he'd run fifty-five. In the weight room, we'd do a set of two hundred twenty-five, he would slide on 2.5's and do a set of two hundred thirty. Finally, one day I was like, 'Hey man, what's the deal? Five pounds? What is five pounds ever going to do for you?' He said, 'Look around. Everyone in here is younger, cheaper, and healthier than me. Everyone in here is here to take my job. The only reason I'm still here is because I come in here, and I steal an inch each and every day. Because an inch leads to a yard, a yard to a first down, a first down to a touchdown, a touchdown to a win—and wins get you an opportunity to go to the Super Bowl.' That was his motto; that was what everything was driving toward. I began to look at it. How do I translate inches into my money? Well, maybe it was while I was out at dinner. Did I get a drink, or did I just get water? Save that inch. But the most important way I translated football to finance with this inch philosophy is through the eighth wonder of the world. Albert Einstein deemed the eighth wonder of the world compound interest because it is an aggregation of inches, an aggregation of small victories. Each day, you can't win the Super Bowl; you can't even get a win. But each day you can steal an inch and make it go to work for you. Each dollar you employ and tell to go work for you, they go out and create their own employees. The power of compound interest is inches adding up to more inches."

—JEDIDIAH COLLINS, CFP® AND FORMER NFL PLAYER

THE POWER OF TIME

Janet and Ted are twins. Both are twenty years old and have hopes of retiring at age sixty-five. One day, they discuss investing. Ted wants to enjoy his youth for a few years before he begins investing, but Janet decides to begin investing today. Janet tells Ted she only plans to invest until she turns thirty-five, at which point she will not contribute any more money to her investments. Ted scoffs, as he tells Janet he will contribute double what she does from age thirty-five to age sixty-five. He urges her to wait to invest until she earns a higher salary. Janet bets Ted she will have a larger nest egg come retirement.

Ted invests *twice* as much as Janet. When retirement arrives, who wins the bet, Janet or Ted?

	Janet	Ted
Age they begin investing	20	35
Age by which they are finished adding contributions	35	65
Annual contributions	$1,000	$1,000
Total amount invested	$15,000	$30,000
Annual rate of return	7%	7%
Money at age 65	$219,006	$101,073

Whoa! Despite the fact Janet saves and invests half the amount Ted does, she has double the money! She earns $117,933 more than him and wins the bet. How did she know she would end up with a larger nest egg? Well, unlike Ted, Janet was familiar with a concept called the *time value of money* (TVM).

The underlying principle of TVM is a dollar in your wallet today is worth more than a dollar in the future because of its growth potential. Time has the power to increase the value of your dollar. Each dollar you invest now could turn into two dollars, then three dollars, then four dollars, and so forth over time. The earlier you start investing and taking advantage of compound growth, the more money you will make. If compound interest is a rocket ship, then time is fuel.

Warren Buffett was able to grasp the importance of time from an early age. "The way numbers exploded as they grew at a constant rate over time was how a small sum could turn into a fortune," wrote Alice Schroeder in her biography of Buffett. "He could picture the numbers compounding as vividly as the way a snowball grew when he rolled it across the lawn." When he was young, Buffett's friends and family would hear him mutter things like, "Do I really want to spend $30,000 on this haircut?" when deciding whether to spend a few dollars. To him, a few dollars that day meant hundreds of thousands of dollars in the future because they could not compound.[31]

THE RULE OF 72

Imagine you are deciding whether to stash $100 in a bank account or invest it in the stock market. You want to figure out approximately how long it will take your money to double. A tool called the Rule of 72 can help you. Simply divide seventy-two by an average annual growth rate. For example, to see how long it will take to double your money in a bank account earning a 2 percent interest rate, simply divide seventy-two by two. Your answer? It will take thirty-six years to double your dollars. Now, how long would it take you to double your Benjamin earning the stock market's average annual 7 percent real return? Divide seventy-two by seven, and you will find it will take around ten years for your $100 to turn into $200.

***

Interest is a core financial concept; it relates to banking, credit cards, debt, and investing. We will explore these

---

31   Jason Zweig, "Warren Buffett and the $300,000 Haircut," *The Wall Street Journal*, August 28, 2020.

applications in different chapters. As you've learned in this chapter, compounding is powerful and can either work *for* you or *against* you. We drew from the inspirational wisdom of Albert Einstein to learn how compound interest can grow your savings exponentially and set you on a path to financial freedom. On the other hand, you also began to understand that if you are a borrower, compound interest can work against you and set you on a financially dangerous path, so it is critical to borrow carefully. However, the biggest takeaway from this chapter is that you have one powerful (yet finite) advantage on your financial journey: time! If you have the psychological hurdle of "I'm young, so I have plenty of time before I need to begin," hopefully this chapter showed you that time is indispensable when it comes to building wealth. The best time to put your money to work for you was yesterday; the second-best time is today. The more money you invest and the longer you let it grow, the more you will have for your future self! Time is money, and all it takes is a little bit of interest for your dollars to grow.

FUN FACTS
- To find out how long it will take your money to triple, divide 114 by your interest rate. To find out how long it will take to quadruple, divide 144 by your interest rate.
- The Rule of 72 can be applied to population growth calculations. For instance, if a town's population is growing at a 12 percent annual rate, it will take six years for its population to double.

Z NOTES

- Borrowing money is rarely free. Whenever you borrow someone's money, you must pay them back additional money, which is called interest.
- Compound interest is interest earned on both principal and accumulated interest.
- The sooner you put your money to work by investing it, the more you can expect to have down the road.
- Compounding is a double-edged sword; it is great if you are regularly saving and investing money but harmful if you are borrowing money.

CHAPTER 8

Banking Basics

When you picture a bank, what comes to mind? Perhaps you conjure an image of a large, imposing brick building with enormous steel vaults and free lollipops. But how many of us really know what a bank is and how it can help one achieve their financial goals? Once you begin regularly earning and saving, it is important to familiarize yourself with banks. A bank is like a home base for your money.

A bank is a financial institution that accepts deposits and makes loans. Some banks, such as Bank of America and Wells Fargo, have physical branches, while others primarily operate online. Digital banking will be explored a little later in this chapter.

Banks are a critical part of the financial system, but they do not always operate with your wellbeing in mind. Banks are *businesses* with the goal of turning a profit. When you walk into a bank and fork over some money to a teller, it is easy to imagine it being a stored in a lockbox in a back room with your name on it, but that is far from what actually happens.

Let's look at an imaginary example to understand how banks work their monetary magic. Michigan Bank's (MB) customers have collectively deposited $1 million in the bank. These customers earn a 2 percent annual interest rate on their deposits. Each year, the bank doles out $20,000 to its depositors. Meanwhile, several people also take out loans with MB. Usually, the bank has around $850,000 of its depositors' money loaned out. It charges its borrowers an average annual interest rate of 9 percent, meaning that it receives $76,500 per year. To put it together, MB is charging its borrowers 9 percent interest and its depositors are earning 2 percent interest. This 7 percent difference is called the spread. Can you see how MB is profiting? It's raking in significantly more money than it is paying out.

The interest a bank pays you on your deposited money is always less than the interest it collects from borrowers, and this premise is how banks make big bucks. When you deposit money in a bank account, the bank notes the amount of your deposit, and your money changes hands several times. The bank loans your money out to someone else so that it can charge them interest. Plus, banks tend to hit their customers high and low with fees. This revolving door of money is instrumental to how banks operate.

THE BENEFITS OF BANKS

Even though banks are out to make money off you, they are still an excellent and safe place to keep some of your money. Keeping a portion of your earnings in a bank can afford you the following benefits:

- **Liquidity:** You can easily deposit, withdraw, and keep track of money.
- **Safety:** A bank is a secure, low-risk place to park your money. The Federal Deposit Insurance Corporation (FDIC) insures up to $250,000 per person in each of your qualifying bank accounts. If your bank was robbed, for instance, the FDIC would cover up to $250,000 of your account balance.
- **Interest:** Recall that you are the lender when you deposit money in the bank, so the bank will pay you interest on your deposits.
- **Straightforward Fund Transfers:** It is easy to link your bank account to a peer-to-peer payment app and pay your friend back for movie tickets or for dinner. You can also link your bank account to an investment account, which we will discuss in a later chapter. Many banks also enable you to arrange automatic bill payments.

TYPES OF BANK ACCOUNTS

There are several different kinds of accounts you can open at a bank, each with different aspects and features. Here is an overview of the main possibilities you might consider:

CHECKING ACCOUNT

Funds in a checking account are typically used for daily transactions. Checking accounts come with a debit card and checks. You may or may not earn interest on the money you keep in a checking account, and if you do earn interest, it is typically a very low rate. A checking account can be thought of as an "everyday" account, as the money in it is typically used for transactions like purchasing birthday gifts and paying for gas.

SAVINGS ACCOUNT

A savings account is just that—an account in which you save money. A high-yield savings account, which pays more interest than a traditional savings account, is a great place to keep your emergency fund. As the funds in a savings account are not meant to be used for daily expenditures, this is not an account from which you frequently withdraw. You generally receive more interest on the money you stash in a savings account than in a checking account, but your money is not as accessible as the dollars you have in a checking account because the account doesn't come with a debit card. Additionally, the bank may place a cap on monthly transactions. A savings account can be thought of as a "future" account, as it is not intended for daily use but rather to set aside funds for your future self.

MONEY MARKET ACCOUNT

A money market account is like a hybrid of a savings and checking account. Money market accounts usually have higher interest rates than savings accounts, typically come with checks and a debit card, and usually allow you six monthly transfers or withdrawals. They often have minimum balance requirements, meaning you must maintain a certain account balance.

CERTIFICATE OF DEPOSIT (CD)

A certificate of deposit is a savings vehicle. You hand over a certain amount of money and are unable to access it for a fixed period of time (several months or years). The interest rates associated with CDs are much higher than those associated with traditional savings accounts. The longer the term of your CD, the higher the interest rate you earn, as the bank can loan your money out for a longer period of time and generate more money with it. For example, a five-year CD typically earns interest at a higher rate than a three-year CD. Early withdrawals from a CD trigger a penalty.

CREDIT UNIONS

Credit unions are similar to banks but differ greatly in one way: they prioritize serving their members over generating profits. While banks are for-profit institutions, credit unions are not-for-profit institutions. Just like a bank, you can deposit money into accounts at a credit union and take out loans. However, you may receive better interest rates, lower loan rates, and lower fees.

BANK ACCOUNTS AT A GLANCE

FACTORS TO CONSIDER WHEN PICKING A BANK ACCOUNT

- **Transaction Limits/Fund Accessibility**—How frequently can funds be withdrawn from the account?
- **Fees**—Are there any fees associated with the account? If so, what are they and how are they incurred?
- **Minimum Balance Requirement**—Is there a certain amount of money required to open the account? Does a certain account balance need to be maintained?
- **Interest Rate**—What is the interest rate on deposits in the account?

COMMON FEES

- Using an ATM that is not affiliated with your bank
- *Overdrafts* (completing a transaction that makes your account balance negative)
- Wire transfers
- Too many transactions (many banks limit the number of withdrawals you can make per month from certain accounts)

BOUNCING CHECKS

When you cut a check, the person or company to which you write it might not immediately cash it. Let's say John wrote Haley a $150 check in January for her birthday. At the time, John had a $400 balance in his account. However, Haley does not cash the check until April when John has a $100 balance. When Haley cashes the check, it bounces. A check bounces when someone attempts to cash a check you wrote them, but the funds in your account are insufficient to cover it. Therefore, it's important to keep track of your deposits and withdrawals. If you withdraw $200 from your account, make a note of it. If your $600 monthly paycheck is deposited in your account, make a note of it. Keeping detailed tabs can prevent you from shelling out a fee.

AUTOMATED TELLER MACHINES (ATMS)

An ATM is the digital equivalent of a human bank teller. Using an ATM, you can complete simple banking activities, such as checking your account balances and withdrawing cash. ATMs are convenient in that they are often available twenty-four hours per day and can be found internationally.

If you wish to bank in an eco-friendly manner, consider "green" banks and credit unions. These institutions lend out the money you deposit, but they utilize it to support environmental and social causes. For example, the Clean Energy Credit Union helps consumers afford clean energy products and services, such as electric vehicles and net-zero energy homes. Aspiration Bank gives you cashback when you shop with socially conscious retailers. Learn more at greenamerica.org/getabetterbank.

DIGITAL BANKING

Banking is undergoing a massive digital disruption. Many people no longer want (or need) to trek to a physical bank branch to handle their banking business when they can take care of it with a few taps on their phones from anywhere, anytime. Plus, digital banking offers useful features, such as the ability to receive text notifications from your bank when your account balance is low to minimize the risk of overdrafts. In essence, digital banking is convenient, quick, and appealing to our digitally native generation. The shift to digital banking was greatly accelerated by the COVID-19 pandemic. April 2020 saw a 200 percent jump in new mobile banking registrations, and mobile banking traffic rose 85 percent. In a survey by fintech company Novantas, only 40 percent of respondents said they expected to return to physical bank branches post-pandemic.[32]

You can complete digital banking activities via a bank's mobile app or website. Pioneered by Capital One and Bank of America, voice-based banking is burgeoning. Capital One's Eno monitors your account and helps prevent fraud. Bank of America's Erica is a virtual financial assistant whose capabilities range from paying bills to providing a weekly spending snapshot.

Digital banking activities often include:

- Paying bills
- Viewing account balances
- Applying for credit cards
- Depositing checks
- Transferring money
- Arranging recurring transfers from one bank account to another
- Locating ATMs and physical bank branches

---

32 Ellen Sheng, "Coronavirus Crisis Mobile Banking Is a Shift That's Likely to Stick," *CNBC*, May 27, 2020.

***

Opening a bank account is the cornerstone of your financial journey. Once you begin regularly saving and earning money, you need a place to stash your dollars other than your t-shirt drawer. I remember when I opened my first bank account when I was ten years old. I loved to carry around the little ledger I received. I felt empowered. Creating a bank account opens you up to a wide range of possibilities. Once you do so, you can begin to invest. The face of banking is rapidly evolving as society enters a fully digital era. Banking may look very different in ten years than it does today.

FUN FACTS
- Banca Monte dei Paschi in Siena, Italy, is the world's oldest bank and dates back to 1472.
- Prized linked savings accounts encourage people to save through gamification. They function similarly to traditional savings products but give customers the chance to enter raffles for cash prizes by making deposits into their account.

Z NOTES
- A bank is generally a great place to keep a portion of your money. You can easily keep track of it, it is protected by the FDIC, and you may even earn a little bit of interest.

- Banks are businesses. When you deposit money at a bank, the bank often lends it to other people to charge them interest. The interest a bank pays you on the money you deposit is always less than what it charges borrowers.
- Digital banking is a very relevant topic for Gen Z. This industry will only see more growth in the coming years, and it is making it easier to bank anywhere, anytime.

CHAPTER 9

Borrowing Benjamins: Credit and Debt

———

"How Student Debt Became a $1.6 Trillion Crisis." "5 Life Mile-stones Millennials Are Delaying Because of Student Loan Debt." Gen Z grew up surrounded by headlines like these and hearing horror stories about the massive amounts of debt millennials took on. But do we really understand what debt is and how it can impact one's ability to achieve financial independence?

Debt is borrowed money. If you borrow twenty dollars from your friend, you become indebted to her. As you learned in Chapter 7, you often have to pay someone interest when you borrow their money. When a bank or credit card company lends you money and you have to pay them the amount you borrowed plus interest, you are taking on debt. When you take out a student loan, you are taking on debt. Because credit cards are fast and convenient, using them is an easy way to accrue debt if you aren't careful.

CREDIT CARDS VS. DEBIT CARDS

Imagine you are eating lunch out at a restaurant with your friends. You pull out your wallet, look inside, and see you have two different payment options. You can either pay with your debit card or with your credit card. Hmm . . . which to choose? This seemingly small dilemma actually matters a lot.

You recall a friend telling you something about being able to take a free vacation with airplane miles. Cash back sure sounds nice. Plus, you've heard that you can build your credit score by using a credit card. Sounds great, right? However, it could also be, as I said before, that there is more to this choice than what meets the eye. To make the best decision for yourself, you need to understand how your two payment options differ. Let's dive right in.

Your meal costs fifteen dollars. You stand at the cash register and stall, thinking about the differences between the seemingly identical pieces of plastic. If you swipe your debit card, you will be directly withdrawing some of the money in your bank account to pay for your lunch. If you don't have enough money in your bank account, your transaction will not go through. Let's say you currently have a seventy-five-dollar balance in your account. As your debit card is linked to your bank account, you will have a sixty-dollar account balance after the transactions goes through (seventy-five dollars minus fifteen dollars).

Meanwhile, if you swipe your credit card, your credit card company will receive a notification that you are requesting money to pay for your lunch. The company will pay the restaurant on your behalf and send a charge to your account.

In this context, using a credit card means you receive money now and agree to repay it later. After you swipe your credit card, you will still have a seventy-five-dollar balance in your bank account. Your balance is the amount of money you owe the credit card company. When you receive your bill, you should repay the credit company to avoid accruing interest. Your $15 transaction will be reflected in your credit card statement along with your other expenditures.

CREDIT CARD	DEBIT CARD
• Enables you to purchase items now and pay for them later	• Uses funds from your bank account
• Can build good credit if you pay on time or bad if you don't	• Does not impact credit history
• May earn rewards and/or points if you spend a certain sum of money	• No rewards
• Pay interest on unpaid balance	• No interest

ALL ABOUT CREDIT CARDS

A credit card is a convenient payment option. Nearly all retailers and merchants accept credit cards, so you can charge them virtually anywhere. Credit cards offer a layer of security and fraud protection. Additionally, when used properly, they can build your credit score. We will talk about credit scores later in this chapter, but, put simply, your credit score reflects your creditworthiness. It is not just useful for potential lenders, though. Landlords often consider your credit score when deciding whether or not to rent to you. Kelly DiGonzini, director of financial planning at Beacon Pointe, recommends, "Use a credit card but only for everyday things you would pay cash for, and pay off your full balance at the end of every month. That builds your credit."

Some credit companies attempt to entice you by offering you free cash or points when you use their cards. Who doesn't love free money? But it's important to take a step back. How can credit card companies (which are businesses) afford to give you *free* money? Offering you free cash back is meant to incentivize you to rack up a lot of charges to your credit card. You have to spend a large sum of money with your credit card to get that free cash. Imagine you earn 3 percent cash back on your credit card. To earn $15, you must spend $500 (.03 x 500). It's one thing if you spend the $500 on something you need and can afford, but it's another if you waste $500 on things you don't need just to receive fifteen bucks. When the credit card company offers you rewards, they do so knowing that you might very well spend more than you can afford to get the rewards and will then be unable to pay your full balance at the end of the month. Then, they can charge you interest on your unpaid balance. The interest they receive is much greater in comparison to the rewards they dole out. There is no such thing as free lunch. The free dessert the company is offering you will soon cost much more than the entire meal!

Credit cards make it very easy to spend on items you cannot truly afford. Just swipe or tap and go! This is the true definition of instant gratification. We all know the surge of endorphins that comes after purchasing something we really wanted. The money you are spending when using a credit card doesn't seem real because you are not physically holding it when you are making a purchase. You tell yourself, "Go ahead because I deserve it. Viva la vida!" However, credit cards are not just pieces of shiny plastic with your name engraved on them; they represent real money. If you spend more than you can afford, you won't be able to pay off your credit card balance in full each month. If you don't pay off your balance in full and on time, credit companies will charge you very high interest rates.

The interest rate you will be charged over the course of one year on a carried balance is called an *annual percentage rate (APR)*. If your APR was hypothetically 16 percent and you had a fifty-dollar balance for a year, you would be charged eight dollars (.16 x 50) that year. You can determine your monthly rate by dividing your annual rate by twelve. Sixteen percent APR = 16 percent/twelve months = 1.33 percent per month. You incur APR charges when you only pay the minimum due on your credit card, as you carry a balance past the due date.

Let's look at an example of how paying the minimum due on your credit card can dig you into a deep hole of debt. Imagine twenty-one-year-old Michael is deciding whether to purchase the latest $1,100 iPhone. He recently saw an advertisement that said that he could receive the item today and only pay a few bucks per month for it. What an amazing deal—he can begin using his new smartphone today and doesn't have to drain his wallet.

Clearly, Michael doesn't understand how to use a credit card responsibly. Let's examine his case. Michael buys a new iPhone for $1,100 with his credit card, meaning he has a $1,100 balance. His credit card company charges him an 18 percent annual interest rate. For the sake of simplicity, assume his monthly minimum payment is twenty dollars. How long will it take him to pay off his balance by making the minimum payment each month?

Month	Beginning	Interest	Minimum Due	End
1	$1,100	$16.50	$20	$1,096.50
2	$1,097	$16.45	$20	$1,093.45
3	$1,093.45	$16.40	$20	$1,089.85
4	$1,089.85	$16.35	$20	$1,086.20
5	$1,086.20	$16.29	$20	$1,082.49
6	$1,082.49	$16.24	$20	$1,078.73
7	$1,078.73	$16.18	$20	$1,074.91
8	$1,074.91	$16.12	$20	$1,071.03
9	$1,071.03	$16.07	$20	$1,067.10
10	$1,067.10	$16.01	$20	$1,063.11
11	$1,063.11	$15.95	$20	$1,059.06
12	$1,059.06	$15.89	$20	$1,054.95

At the end of one year, Michael has only reduced his credit card balance by around forty-five dollars. How much has he shelled out in interest payments? $194. Yes, he is certainly losing money and has barely made a dent in his balance. Notice how the interest that he pays each month only decreases by a few cents. Remember when we talked about how compound interest can either help or hurt you in Chapter 7? Well, using credit cards improperly is a prime example of how it can financially harm you if you aren't prudent. Paying the minimum amount that you owe often means you will continue to pay the credit company interest for years after your initial purchase. If he continues only paying the minimum due, Michael will end up paying $1,241 in interest. It will take him nearly eleven years and eight months to pay off his balance. He will pay significantly more for the iPhone than it originally cost. Of course, this would be a different situation if Michael bought the iPhone on his credit card and paid his balance off quickly and in full. Even if he paid forty dollars each month, he would pay $329 in interest over the course of three years.

SPEND PRUDENTLY

Remember this cardinal rule: only purchase what you can truly afford, and if you use a credit card, pay the full balance each month. If you follow this rule, you will not only better your financial health by building your credit score but will also garner the rewards the credit card company may be offering. In general, it is wise to remember creditors and banks will lend you much more money than you can afford to pay back in a timely manner so they can profit by charging you interest. A credit card company hopes you overspend and charge more to your card than you can afford to pay off at the end of the month. In fact, before certain laws were passed, credit card company representatives used to visit college campuses and incentivize students with items like free t-shirts to open a credit card. They knew college students tend to be big spenders. *You* must be disciplined and responsible for your own spending.

Andrew Ross Sorkin, anchor of CNBC's *Squawk Box*, *New York Times* columnist, and bestselling author, claims, "I am a huge believer in this. Do not take on debt. If you can avoid debt, that is the most important thing you can do. Pay your credit card balances. There's a lot of people who have something they want to purchase and take on debt because of it. Save early, save often, put money in [the market] constantly. Keep it in for twenty, thirty, forty years. I would be planning to invest in the stock market over time, buying indexes and holding them, and taking the long-term view."

Money guru Neale Godfrey, one of the first female executives at Chase Bank and author of twenty-seven books pertaining to raising financially responsible kids, was a regular figure on TV. She reminisced about one of the interviews she conducted, "There was a college student who was graduating with $19,000 worth of debt. I did an interview in her apartment, and I was sitting on a yoga ball because she had no furniture. As I balanced on the exercise ball, I asked her, 'What do you really want?' I thought she was going to say furniture. She replied, 'I really wanted a motorcycle.' I said okay. She had $19,000 in credit card debt, and the debt was from stupid purchases. I went over the bills with her. It was pizzas and juices and coffees and worthless stuff. It was going to take her five years to pay it off, by the way, and she would have to pay almost double what the original purchases cost because she was paying about 20 percent on the credit card. On air, I had one curtain behind which was tons of pizza boxes, juice cartons, and empty coffee cups. Behind the other was the motorcycle. We opened the curtains, pointed to the piles of boxes, and said, 'You could have this, which was your choice, or you could have the motorcycle.' She just stood there shocked. The audience gasped, and she broke down into tears. That wasn't my goal, though. I just wanted to show her the impact of our choices. It was so vivid to her. This is what she *decided* to do."

GRACE PERIODS

A *grace period* is the gap between the end of your billing cycle and when your credit card payment is due. After the grace period ends, you will be charged interest. If you do not carry a balance following the grace period, you do not have to pay interest. Remember, credit card companies can *only* charge you if you carry a balance. It is required by law that your credit card companies make your statement available to you at least twenty-one days before the due date.

HOW TO AVOID BECOMING ENSNARED IN THE JAWS OF CREDIT CARD DEBT:

- Never spend more than you can afford.
- Avoid a *cash advance.* A cash advance is a short-term loan from your credit card company. It often comes with hefty fees and an interest rate higher than your APR. In taking out this loan, you do not receive a grace period and begin to accumulate interest immediately.
- Do not just pay the minimum amount due. The credit card company profits when you only repay a fraction of what you owe. However, over time, doing so can mean you end up paying significantly more for an item than it originally cost. Pay off your entire balance on time each month.
- Set a *spending limit* on your credit card. A spending limit is the maximum balance you are able to charge to your card. Establishing a limit can help remind you that the sky is not the limit.

- Keep your *credit utilization ratio* below 30 percent. Your credit utilization ratio is your outstanding credit card balances divided by all your credit card limits. If you have $5,000 of available credit on five separate cards, aim to spend no more than $1,500 (30 percent x $5,000) in total. Additionally, avoid maxing out a single card (reaching your credit limit).
- Automate your credit card payment.

"GOOD" DEBT AND "BAD" DEBT

There are two sides to every story. Although debt can put you in a financially precarious position, some types can also help you achieve your goals. "Good" debt is that which may help you increase your net worth down the road. The main types of "good" debt are mortgages and student loans. Houses tend to increase in value over time, so taking out a mortgage can be a good investment. Student loans may enable you to obtain an education which results in a job with a high salary. We've already explored the main type of "bad" debt—credit card debt—throughout this chapter. Let's explore types of "good" debt in greater depth.

MORTGAGES

Because many people are unable to afford purchasing a house entirely in cash, banks offer mortgages. Typically, borrowers must immediately contribute a lump sum called a *down payment*, which is a percentage of the price of the house. Then, they have to repay the loan through incremental payments over a specified period of time. The interest rates on mortgages tend to be low, and the value of homes tend to increase over time. The two main factors that determine the price of a monthly mortgage payment are the price of the home and the term of the loan. In general, the lower the price of the home and the longer the loan term, the lower the monthly payment. A mortgage is an example of a secured loan. A secured loan is backed by an asset, or **collateral**. Collateral minimizes risk for a lender because if you do not make payments as agreed, it can seize and sell your asset to diminish its financial losses. The house is the collateral for a mortgage.

Let's say you want to purchase your first house, which costs $350,000, but can't afford to pay this sum at one time, so you apply for a mortgage with your bank. After determining that you are creditworthy, the bank approves you for a mortgage. You make a down payment of $70,000, and the bank issues you a loan of $280,000. Each month over a thirty-year period, you repay the loan with a little bit of interest.

FINANCING YOUR EDUCATION

Deciding how to pursue higher education is a consequential decision. Specifically, it is a big *financial* decision and often a stressful one. The cost of higher education is rising every year. Many individuals find themselves needing to take out student loans. People may receive student loans from the federal government, from private sources such as a bank, or from other organizations. The Resources Guide at the end of this book includes websites to help you explore options for funding a college education.

CBS News business analyst, CFP®, and author of *The Dumb Things Smart People Do with Their Money* Jill Schlesinger reflects, "I think the biggest mistake that follows people for a long time is their choice around higher education. It is incredibly important to get a college degree. We know that; it pays benefits over the course of the decades you work. As a college graduate, you will earn more money than your peers who don't attend college. However, it is important to make sure you and your family are not accumulating so much debt that the difference in earning power is simply going toward paying down a loan. I have heard from far too many young adults that the choices they made around college have followed and haunted them for a long time. So, when you're looking ahead and you're looking at college, college makes sense. However, it is also imperative that you run the numbers and make sure you don't accumulate too much debt to get that degree."

PAYING OFF DEBT
There is no one-size-fits-all approach to tackling debt. However, it is typically best to begin by getting organized. Make a list of all your debts, as well as their corresponding interest rate and balance. There are two common strategies for tackling debt:

- Snowball Method: pay off your smallest balances first while making minimum payments on the rest of your debts.
- Avalanche Method: pay the minimum dues on all your debts but put the most money toward the debt with the highest interest rate.

One approach is to try to contact the companies to which you owe money and ask to be put on a payment plan with a lower interest rate. You may also consider a balance transfer.

A balance transfer entails transferring high-interest debt to a new credit card that charges low or no interest for a certain window. Your new credit card company pays off your debt to your old credit card company, and you begin to repay your new credit card company. The catch is that if you are unable to pay off your debt entirely during the introductory period, you may end up with a very high interest rate. Plus, when you initiate a balance transfer, you often have to pay a fee which is a percentage of the balance you want to transfer. You can use a balance transfer calculator to see if this method makes sense for you.

Remember Lauryn William's advice in the "Saving Savvy" chapter? Pay yourself first. This concept also applies for debt. View your debt repayment as you would rent or utilities—a fixed cost. Consider automating your debt payments. Whichever strategy you use to tackle your debt, ensure you have a plan.

UNDERSTANDING CREDIT REPORTS AND CREDIT SCORES

CREDIT REPORTS
Private agencies called credit bureaus keep track of your credit history. There are three main credit bureaus: Equifax, Experian, and TransUnion. Lenders report information about how much you borrow and whether you repay debts on time to the credit bureaus. The credit bureaus keep track of everything that is reported to them, both positive and negative. For example, they take note of your applications for credit cards and of late payments. They compile that information

into credit reports. After seven years, negative information is deleted from your credit reports. You are entitled to a free report from each of the three main credit bureaus, at your request, once per year. Prospective employers might request a modified credit report for insight into your credit history, as how you manage your money can indicate whether you are responsible. Your credit reports are also important because they determine your credit scores.

CREDIT SCORES

A credit score is reflective of your ability to manage money. Think of it as a measure of your financial health. Every person has multiple credit scores. However, of these, FICO is the most recognized. FICO scores are on a scale from 300–850. A high score is reflective of good financial health; creditors feel confident you will repay your future debts as agreed, which translates to favorable loan terms. You will likely need to borrow money at some point. When that time comes, it is beneficial to have a good credit score because it can qualify you for better interest rates on loans, which means you will have more money in your pocket to save and invest. For a thirty-year fixed mortgage with a $250,000 loan principal in April 2021, a 620-639 FICO score equated to a 4.265 percent interest rate and around $193,537 total interest paid, while a 760-850 FICO score equated to a 2.676 percent interest rate and around $113,899 total interest paid.[33] That's a $79,638 total difference, and a $221 difference in terms of monthly payments. Imagine what you could do with that extra money!

---

33   "Loan Savings Calculator," myFico.

Plus, as mentioned before in this chapter, landlords often use your credit scores in deciding whether to rent to you. Just as your GPA reduces your academic record to a single number, your credit score consolidates your financial history into a single number. I encourage you to play around with an online simulator that shows you how altering information in your credit report impacts your credit score.

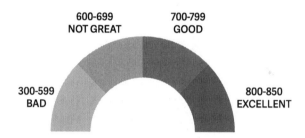

There are five factors that primarily determine your FICO score, with some components carrying more weight than others.

FACTORS

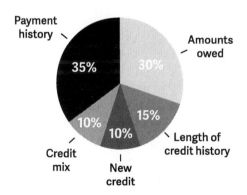

Element	Weighting	Description
Payment history	35%	When considering extending credit to you, the first thing that a lender wants to know is whether you have a pattern of making payments on time, including bill payments, student loan payments, and credit card payments.
Amounts owed	30%	Lenders want to ensure that you are not overextended. Do you max out your credit cards (reach the credit limit)? A credit utilization ratio of less than 30 percent overall and on each individual card demonstrates responsibility.
Length of credit history	15%	How long is your credit history? In general, the longer, the better.
Credit mix	10%	How many different types of credit have you managed? A mix of credit demonstrates that you can handle multiple types of loans. Of course, don't take on debt unless you need to; you do not need to have student loans, a mortgage, and an auto loan to build a high credit score.
New credit	10%	Do you use new credit prudently? Applying for several credit cards in a short period of time generally means you are a high risk for lenders.[34]

Here are a few rules of thumb to follow to optimize your credit score:

- Pay off your credit card balance in full and on time each month.
- Pay all your bills on time.
- Do not use more than 30 percent of your credit limit on any card.
- Avoid closing old credit cards.

---

34 "How are FICO Scores Calculated?" myFico.

***

Misusing credit cards is one of the most common ways that people dig themselves into a deep financial hole. Compound interest is wonderful when it is working for you, but terrible when it is working against you. Unfortunately, the vicious cycle of debt can begin with a few purchases. If you purchase something you cannot afford and carry a balance, you have to pay interest. As you must dedicate money to chipping away at this interest, you may have to take on debt to purchase the items that you do need.

However, it is important to build credit because you will likely need to borrow money at some point. Having good credit qualifies you for lower interest rates and favorable loan terms. The less interest you have to pay, the better.

During the COVID-19 crisis, I interviewed Andrew Ross Sorkin, *New York Times* award winning columnist, anchor of CNBC's *Squawk Box*, and author of *Too Big to Fail*. I asked him whether he thought that, aside from the turmoil caused by the pandemic, another major recession similar to the 2008 financial crisis would ever occur again. He thoughtfully replied, "I imagine something will happen, whether in my lifetime or not. But the lesson of all financial crises is the same: Debt is the match that lights the fire."

FUN FACTS

- The Equal Credit Opportunity Act, which was enacted in 1974, banned lenders from discriminating against credit applicants on the basis of race, marital status, sex, age, and nationality.
- In 1949, businessman Frank McNamara was dining out in New York when he realized he forgot his wallet at home. Luckily, his wife paid his way, but the experience gave McNamara an idea. What if there was a way to purchase a meal on credit and pay for it by the end of the month? Frank and his partners developed the idea for the Diners Club card, which became the first contemporary credit card.

Z NOTES

- Debt is money owed by one party to another.
- Credit cards and debit cards may look similar, but they have significant differences. Spending with a credit card means you are spending borrowed money you will have to repay later, while spending with a debit card means you are spending money from your bank account. Credit cards impact your credit score while debit cards do not.
- Always pay off your credit card balance on time and in full each month. Paying the minimum amount due on your credit card balance means you could continue to pay the credit card company interest for years.
- Only spend what you can truly afford.

- "Good" debt has the potential to increase your net worth, while "bad" debt does not create long-term value.
- Your credit report is used to calculate your credit score.
- A high credit score is reflective of good financial health; lenders feel confident that you are a responsible borrower and will repay your future debts as agreed, which translates to favorable loan terms.
- A good credit score can qualify you for lower interest rates on loans.

PART 3

INVESTING IN YOURSELF

CHAPTER 10

Buy Low, Sell High: An Introduction to the Stock Market

———

"We often say you have to be wealthy to invest. That's not true, but you do have to invest to be wealthy."

—*FARNOOSH TORABI*

In 1944, Anne Scheiber invested $5,000 in the stock market. When she passed away at the age of 101 in 1995, Scheiber had amassed a fortune of $22 million, which she donated in its entirety to Yeshiva University.[35]

Scheiber's path to wealth was not complicated. She was not a professional investor nor a trust fund baby and did not earn an extraordinarily high salary; she was an auditor at

---

35 James Glassman, "An Old Lady's Lesson: Patience Usually Pays" *Washington Post*, December 17, 1995.

the IRS. In fact, if we exercise the same discipline and follow the same basic principles Anne Scheiber did, you and I could potentially replicate her success and amass our own fortunes through investing.

Scheiber invested in companies she believed in and with which she was familiar. Well-known companies like Coca Cola and Pfizer made up a large portion of her portfolio. She was not by any means a professional investor, but Scheiber paid attention to her companies. She attended their shareholder meetings and reinvested the dividends she received to purchase more shares of stock.

Exercising patience and discipline, Scheiber took a long-term approach to her investing. Instead of buying stocks one week and selling them the next—as many people do fruitlessly—she held her investments for several years and maintained discipline through downturns and turbulent periods. If Scheiber had only lived until age seventy or eighty, she would likely have nowhere near $22 million. Time coupled with discipline allowed her money to grow. Imagine if you began investing today—in your teens, twenties, or thirties.

WHY INVEST?

COMPOUND INTEREST

Let's say Josh is a twenty-four-year-old living in California earning the state's average after-tax income (as of 2020), which is $60,031.[36] This equates to approximately $5,000

---

36   John Csiszar, "How Much You Take Home from the Average Salary in Each State," *Yahoo Finance*, October 13, 2020.

per month. Josh invests 10 percent of his salary in the stock market—$500 per month, every month, for forty-one years until he is sixty-five years old (with a little bit of gray hair) and ready to retire. If he earned the stock market's average annual real return of 7 percent, he would have accumulated $1,421,722 through investing alone. This sum of money is equivalent to what he earned working for over twenty-three-and-a-half years (more than half of his career). In other words, if he didn't invest, he would have to work until he was eighty-eight-and-a-half years old to accumulate the same amount of money. If Josh invested 10 percent of his salary, he would retire a *millionaire*.

> "*If you don't find a way to make money while you sleep, you will work until you die.*"
>
> —*WARREN BUFFETT*

Andrew Ross Sorkin advises, "Start investing now." He explains, "The most common money mistakes I see young people making is they live beyond their means, they don't save, and they don't invest because they think, 'I'm young. I have time. I can just do it later.'" As you learned in Chapter 7, you have the most powerful force in the world on your side as a young person: time.

INFLATION

Is there a restaurant or store you and your family have been going to since you were a little kid? Have you ever noticed how the price of its food or merchandise has gradually increased over time? If so, it may be due to *inflation*. Inflation is the gradual increase in the price of goods and services over time and the concomitant decrease in purchasing power. Historically, the value of the dollar has decreased 2–3 percent per year. This may mean the salad you always get at your favorite café was ten dollars five years ago and twelve dollars today. Just think about how much more expensive a cup of coffee from Starbucks is today compared to a few years ago. In December 2020, one hundred dollars had the same buying power as seventy-three dollars and six cents in December 2004.[37]

Inflation occurs because money doesn't have an anchor. Dollars are not fixed to real assets like gold and land, which are finite. When the government prints more money, the value of the US dollar decreases. This means even if you keep your hard-earned dollars in a high-yield savings account earning 2 percent interest, inflation erodes the value of your savings.

THE RISK AND RETURN BALANCE
When it comes to investing, it is critical to understand that risk and return go hand in hand. The higher the risk, the greater the potential for reward. For example, if you stash your cash in your mattress, your money is very secure but has no potential to grow. In fact, the value of your money declines over time without you even touching it due to inflation. You take on no risk but have no potential for reward. On the other hand, if you take a spring break trip to Vegas

---

37 "CPI Inflation Calculator," US Bureau of Labor Statistics.

and spend your money during a lively night playing poker in a hotel lobby, you have a slim chance of striking it big but virtually no security. You take on an extremely high degree of risk for the potential of an astronomical return.

My guess is you want to earn a return on your dollars without taking on excessive risk. Your safest realistic option would be to store your money in a bank account and earn a low return on it. You could put your money in a CD, which we discussed a bit in Chapter 8. As a reminder, a CD is a savings vehicle that has a fixed term. Money parked in a CD typically earns a higher interest rate than that stashed in a savings account. Alternatively, you could invest your money in bonds. A **bond** is essentially a loan an investor makes to a party that needs money (this can be a government, municipality, or corporation). In exchange, the investor receives interest payments.

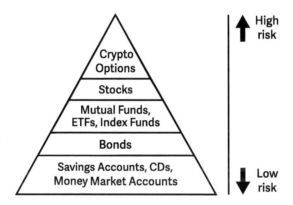

Unfortunately, while all the options listed toward the bottom of the pyramid carry little risk, they are associated with low returns that are often negated by inflation. Saving is the foundation of a good financial plan, but alone it is most likely insufficient to reach your financial goals. If you invested $1,000 every year for forty years in a savings account earning 1 percent interest, you would have around $49,375. If you invested that money and earned the stock market's average annual real return of 7 percent, you would have around $213,610.

Thus, long term, it is important to balance your risk and keep some of your money in the market. Most definitions of risk are focused on the short term; many people measure the risk associated with investing in the stock market by how much an investment fluctuates in price over a few months or a year. However, I maintain that a greater risk is being inhibited from reaching your goals by money. Investing allows you to put your money to work for you. Tim Sheehan, the founder and CEO of Greenlight, remarks, "Investing is how you build true wealth over the long term."

> *"How many millionaires do you know who have become wealthy by investing in savings accounts? I rest my case."*
>
> —ROBERT G. ALLEN

Yes, stocks absolutely have risk associated with them. While some companies increase in value, others perform poorly and go out of business. However, there are ways to mitigate your risk that I will present to you in the following chapters. The problem is that not investing can be risky. Over the long term, the overall stock market has continually gone up. Of course, your investments won't perform well every single day; the market frequently surges and dips. As a whole, though, the market has always trended upward.

Stocks have historically had an annual *real* return of 7 percent. "Real return" is the return after factoring in inflation. Before factoring in inflation, stocks have historically had around a 10 percent annual return.

AVERAGE ≠ NORMAL

As I alluded to, it's important to grasp that the average market performance is not normal. What does that mean? Don't expect to earn a 7 percent return on your investments every year. The value of your investments might increase 17 percent one year and fall by 12 percent the next. This unguaranteed performance is why you should keep emergency money in a savings account with a good interest rate and plan to invest money in the stock market for the long-term. Again, over time you will make significant gains in the stock market, making it an excellent place to grow long-term wealth.

WHAT IS THE STOCK MARKET?

From the moment you wake up to when you turn the lights off at night, you interact with dozens of companies. In the morning before school, you pull on your Nike shoes and grab the textbooks you purchased from Barnes & Noble. Before class, you stop at Starbucks for your morning caffeine boost while jamming to your favorite Spotify playlist. Once you are in school, you Google a question you have during class.

During your morning break, you scroll through Instagram. After school, you attend sports practice and put the gear you purchased from Dick's Sporting Goods to good use. As you drive home after practice, you see tons of Teslas on the road. You suddenly remember that you have to Venmo your friend some money for movie tickets they bought yesterday. Your mind then drifts to spring break vacation. Perhaps you will take a flight with Delta Airlines in a Boeing jet. You can take an Uber to the airport and stay in an Airbnb. Once you get home from practice, you pick up an Amazon package from the front door. Then, you pull out your Apple iPhone and decide to get Chipotle delivered to your home via Doordash. You pay using a debit card issued by Bank of America. Glancing at your phone, you see a reminder email via Microsoft Outlook that you are in charge of bringing team snacks for your next meet—you may need to stop by Target or Walmart tomorrow. You shower and do the dishes, using Procter and Gamble products. Finally, you unwind from a long day with a bit of Netflix . . . it goes on and on.

Stocks allow you to own tiny pieces of the businesses that are seamlessly integrated into your daily life. When you purchase a company's stock, you are purchasing a small piece of that company, which is called a share. A stock represents a share of ownership in a company. Therefore, you become a partial owner of a business when you purchase a share of its stock. When you own stock in a company, you are called a shareholder. The number of shares of a company's stock you hold represents the approximate portion of the company you own. For example, if you own ten shares of a company with ten thousand total shares of stock, you own 0.001 percent of the company.

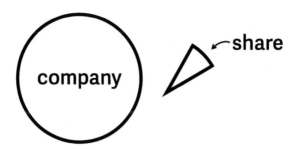

MAKING MONEY WITH STOCKS

Shareholders primarily make money in two ways:

1. **Through price appreciation.** If a shareholder sells shares of stock for more than they paid for them, they profit. For example, imagine you purchase ten shares of Beatific Banana Bread for $100 each, investing a total of $1,000 ($100 x 10 shares). Two years later, your shares are $120 each. They are now collectively worth $1,200 ($120 x 10 shares). Your investment has increased in value by 20 percent. If you sell your shares, you will make $200 ($1200-$1000) and convert the "paper profit" into a tangible profit. You could also hold onto your shares if you believe the company will continue to perform well. Six months later your shares may be worth $107. Or perhaps they'll be worth $128. If they are worth $128, you can sell them for a profit of $280 ($1,280-$1,000). You have the freedom to decide which companies seem to have the most favorable prospects.

2. **Through *dividends*.** Dividends are regular payments that a company makes to its shareholders. These may be paid out in the form of cash or additional stock. Not all companies pay dividends, but those that do typically do so on a quarterly basis. Generally speaking, larger and

well-established companies are more likely to pay dividends than smaller companies that want to invest in their growth. For example, Coca Cola pays dividends.

EXCHANGES

Shares of public companies are bought and sold through stock market exchanges. Exchanges unite buyers and sellers, sort of like a farmers market. Each exchange has its own standards and requirements that govern which companies can be listed on it. A company can list its shares on more than one exchange.

When you want to invest in a company, you can't just visit the exchange and place your order as you would at a restaurant. You must place your stock trades through a brokerage, which acts as a "middleman" and takes care of the exchange on your behalf. Brokerage accounts are offered by many different companies like Fidelity and Charles Schwab. We will discuss brokerages a bit more in Chapter 14.

In the United States, the two main stock exchanges are the Nasdaq and the New York Stock Exchange. Both exchanges are open for trading between 9:30 a.m. and 4 p.m. ET.

THE NASDAQ

Established in 1971, the Nasdaq has many of the largest tech companies in the world listed on it, including Amazon, Apple, Facebook, and Microsoft. A trendsetter, the Nasdaq has established many precedents. It was the first exchange to: offer electronic trading, to store data in the cloud, and to supply its technology to other stock exchanges. The Nasdaq lists more than 3,300 companies. All the Nasdaq's trades occur electronically, as the exchange does not have a physical trading floor.

THE NEW YORK STOCK EXCHANGE

Perhaps you visualize a bunch of men in suits running around a large trading floor and shouting at each other when you hear "investing." Featuring some of the world's largest corporations, the New York Stock Exchange (NYSE) was founded in 1817. It is the largest stock exchange in the world in terms of the total value of all the companies listed on it. For several years, it relied exclusively on physical floor trading, utilizing the open outcry system. As of this writing, the NYSE transitioned to all-electronic trading due to the COVID-19 pandemic.

PUBLIC VS. PRIVATE

You can invest in any company that is "public." When a company is public, it is listed on a stock exchange and anyone is able to trade its shares of stock. The company is referred to as publicly traded. On the other hand, when a company is "private," the general public cannot invest in it.

Companies typically "go public" through a process called an *initial public offering (IPO).* Before an IPO is issued, a company works with underwriters (investment banks) to determine its worth and to figure out how many shares to sell based on a detailed analysis of its profits, operating costs, and other pertinent factors. Once the company goes public, its popularity with investors dictates its stock price. If the company is popular among investors, high demand drives its price up. If it is not, its stock price decreases.

Although there are a few like Chick-fil-A that are not, most large, major companies are public, such as Amazon, Microsoft, Apple, Nike, Walmart, Home Depot, Lululemon, Chipotle, and Starbucks. A company goes public to generate the funds needed to grow its business and increase in value. A company may sell stock to raise money to:

- Develop new products
- Hire more employees
- Expand into new markets

TICKER SYMBOLS

Ticker symbols are abbreviations used to distinguish publicly traded companies. They can consist of numbers, letters, or a combination of both.

NYSE Examples:
JP Morgan: JPM
McDonalds: MCD

NASDAQ Examples:
Petco: WOOF
Lululemon: LULU

HOW STOCK PRICES ARE DETERMINED

Unlike how you purchase an item at a store, you don't buy shares of a company at a fixed price. Stock prices are driven by the interplay between buyers and sellers and investors' perceptions of a company's worth. Let's say Benny's Books is trading at $125. If I think that the company is really worth $160, then $125 seems like a reasonable price. If another investor believes that the company is only worth $99, then he might be inclined to sell. If there is high demand for a stock, then its share price will increase. On the other hand, if more investors are selling a stock than buying, the share price will decrease. The highest price an investor is willing to pay for a stock is called the bid, and the lowest price at which an investor is willing to sell the stock is called the ask. The difference is the bid-ask spread. The demand for a stock depends on several factors, including:

- A company's earnings or profits
- Company-related news and company initiatives
- Future performance expectations
- Economic conditions

For example, a successful product launch might cause the share price of a company's stock to increase, while product recalls or an unexpected change in management might cause a company's share price to drop. Share prices are constantly in flux because the market is pricing in new information.

At the end of each trading day, the closing price of stocks are recorded. The closing price of a stock is generally the last price at which it was trading upon the end of the trading day. Daily closing prices are often viewed as indications of how well a company and the overall market are performing.

INVESTING VS. TRADING

Fundamentally, trading and investing both involve you deploying money into companies with the intent of profiting. However, there are major differences between trading and investing. A trader is sort of like a driver who constantly weaves in and out of lanes. He is in a hurry to reach his destination and takes on risk every time he changes lanes, whereas the driver who stays in a single lane focuses on what is in front of him and often reaches his destination first. Changing lanes frequently also requires a degree of focus and skill.

The objective of traders is to turn a quick profit through capitalizing on the short-term price fluctuations of individual stocks. Trading is significantly riskier than investing. A trader relies on market *volatility* and earns small returns by entering and exiting positions within a short window of time. For example, say that a company has to postpone its rollout of a new product, and its share price falls. It normally trades at around $105, but its price falls to $96. A trader might buy on the dip and sell as soon as the stock rebounds and reaches $109. Meanwhile, an investor focused on the long game would likely barely pay attention to the drop and focus on the company's overall performance and long-term growth prospects. One of the downsides of trading is that it doesn't allow you to reap the benefits of compound interest. Additionally, selling your investments shortly after you purchase them has hefty tax implications (see Chapter 14). Oftentimes, it is wise to focus on time in the market, not timing the market.

"Timing the market . . . is a fool's errand," remarks Karen Finerman, cofounder and CEO of Metropolitan Capital,

New York Times bestselling author, and panelist on CNBC's *Fast Money.*

Timing the market is very risky because nobody can predict the future. The majority of people who day trade frequently end up losing money. Tim Chen, the CEO of Nerdwallet, says, "I lost all my money day trading in college. It's a very cyclical thing. Every ten to twenty years, the stock market goes crazy and then everyone starts to get interested. People dip their toe in the water, they make a bunch of money, they think they're a genius, and they start to do more of it. Then, all of a sudden, they lose all their money. Until I became a professional investor, I didn't really understand there are people who spend vast amounts of money, time, and brain energy trying to beat the system. The amount of data they have is incredible. Some have satellite imagery of parking lots so they can tell how many people there are out shopping. There is no way you are going to get an edge on them. [Day trading] is really like straight up gambling."

At the end of the day, without the expertise and tools, trading is rarely a profitable strategy for rookies. Most successful investors keep their eyes on their long-term financial goals instead of trying to benefit from the minor price shifts of a stock. They take advantage of the fact that the market has historically continued to appreciate throughout history, and they seek companies with strong fundamentals. Additionally, investing for the long-term isn't as time consuming as trading. Trading requires a lot of dedication, as you have to scrupulously research and keep tabs on individual investments and then keep your finger on the metaphorical trigger, ready to buy and sell at a given moment. Investing is not about speculation and hot stock tips. Rather, it is about growing your wealth over time. Though it may sound trite, building wealth in the stock market truly is a marathon—not a sprint.

JJ Kinahan, chief market strategist at TD Ameritrade, advises, "Know the timeframe of your investment. Are you investing in something you think you are going to hold for a year, or are you investing for something you think you are going to hold for a week? If you're only going to hold for a week, little pieces of news are going to have a big effect. If you're going to hold it for a year, you can say, 'Okay, it's moving against me, but I can buy more because I am still a long-term believer.' I think knowing your timeframe is one of the more underrated things people don't normally talk about."

THE ECONOMY AND THE STOCK MARKET

The stock market and the economy are two different entities, but they have an important relationship.

The stock market often reacts to federal economic measures. For example, when the government sends Americans stimulus checks during economic downturns, consumer spending tends to increase, which, in turn, helps businesses thrive. Consumers generally spend more when the economy is healthy, so companies enjoy profits, which pushes the prices of stocks up.

The performance of some companies and industries can depend on the state of the overall economy. Cyclical stocks are those whose prices tend to increase and decrease in accordance with the overall economy. Many of these companies offer discretionary goods and services. Meanwhile, the performance of non-cyclical stocks (also known as "defensive" stocks) is less dependent on the overall health of the economy, so they generally offer investors greater stability. During recessions, defensive stocks tend to do well because people always need to buy things like food and household products. Cyclical stocks tend to stagnate or suffer during recessions because people tend to not travel or make big-ticket purchases, such as cars, quite as much. During the COVID-19 pandemic, the industrial sector, which includes airlines and cruise lines, suffered as people quarantined in their homes. Companies like Walmart and Costco performed well, as families still purchased groceries and toilet paper. As individuals began to get vaccinated, the industrial sector boomed because many people took road trips and deployed their savings on vacations.

There can be disconnects between the stock market's performance and the health of the economy. For example, in 2020, US GDP declined, and millions of Americans were unemployed as a result of the pandemic. However, after a plunge in March, the market boomed and surged, frequently notching record highs, as the government injected large amounts of stimulus into the economy and investors were hopeful that vaccines would soon be available so that we could return to a semblance of normal life. The stock market is forward thinking and is reflective of what investors predict will be happening months in the future, which is why many businesspeople love the famous Wayne Gretzky quote, "Skate to where the puck is going, not where it's been."

WHAT IF I DON'T HAVE ENOUGH MONEY TO INVEST?

I'm willing to bet you have enough money to invest if you are savvy about your spending. I'd like to return to an earlier example from the book and take a look at what would happen if you invested the money you saved from cutting out a couple of small purchases per week. Purchasing two $5 lattes each week equates to around $520 each year (52 weeks x $10). Don't get me wrong—as I have mentioned, I firmly believe you do not need to give up all of life's pleasures to achieve financial independence. However, if you cut out just *one* coffee every week, you would have an extra $260. If you saved $5 per week and invested $20 per month in the stock market for forty years and earned a 7 percent return, you would earn $52,802. Imagine if you drank five $5 coffees per week and invested that money! Whatever you can invest will help you in the long run. Time coupled with compound interest allows small amounts of money to grow into a sizable sum. Luckily, it is easier than ever to take advantage of every penny you have; fractional shares and micro-investing platforms allow you to invest your spare change in the stock market, as you will learn about in Part 4.

Neale Godfrey recounted her grandfather's financial story to me: "He lived during the Great Depression. He had lost a lot of money in the stock market, and it *really* made my grandmother crazy. She made him promise he would never buy another stock in his life. So, he promised. But he would collect pennies here and there. He had this jar he would keep his coins in, and my grandmother never noticed. Then, he would take them down to his broker. My grandfather bought original Xerox and AT&T for *pennies*. My grandmother lived to be one hundred years old, and the stock

Grandpa had bought supported her for her entire life after he died."

Wow. Through investing just pennies, Ms. Godfrey's grandfather was able to support his wife for the rest of her *life* after he passed away. Although pennies are worth less today because of inflation, imagine how much your money could grow if you began investing now. Can you really afford not to invest?

***

What if our generation changed the way we interact with businesses and became owners instead of consumers? What if we profited from the brands we love instead of just the opposite? Through investing in the stock market and owning pieces of the businesses in which we believe, Gen Z can create unparalleled wealth.

FUN FACTS
- A $1,000 investment in Apple on its December 12, 1980 IPO would be worth around $430,000 as of 2018.[38]
- You can invest in real estate, commodities (like gold and oil), art, stamps, and wine.

---

38 Emmie Martin, "If You Invested $1,000 in Apple at its IPO, Here's How Much Money You'd Have Now," *CNBC*, November 1, 2018.

Z NOTES

- When you purchase a stock, you become a partial owner of a company.
- Stock prices are driven by supply and demand.
- Shares of stocks are purchased and sold on a stock exchange. Investors can't directly interact with a stock exchange, so they work with a broker, who acts as a middleman.
- When you invest in the stock market, you hope that the companies you invest in will increase in value over time and eventually be worth more than what you paid for them.
- You can make money investing in stocks through price gains, dividends, or both. If you sell a share of stock on a day when the price of that share is higher than the price you paid for it, you make money. Dividends are portions of a company's earnings distributed to share-holders and can serve as a steady stream of income.
- Any positive or negative news about a company—such as product recalls—could potentially impact its stock price because investors may adjust their opinions of what the stock is worth and subsequently buy or sell.
- Trading and investing both involve deploying money into the stock market with the intent of profiting, but trading involves capitalizing on a stock's short-term price fluctuations with the objective of making quick cash, while investing is more about the long game.
- Investors that stick with their investments for long periods of time have generally been rewarded with strong returns.

CHAPTER 11

Zoomers Just Wanna Have Fun(ds)

"Don't look for the needle in the haystack. Just buy the haystack!"
—JOHN BOGLE

Imagine you and your friends want to host a dinner soirée. You all can either purchase the ingredients and cook the meal yourself, or you can hire an experienced chef to plan the menu, handpick the ingredients, and put together a delicious dinner on your behalf. After deciding that cooking isn't your forte, you and your friends pool your money together to hire the chef. In return for his fee, you expect that he will prepare a delectable meal significantly tastier than what you could have fixed yourself.

This is similar to how a ***mutual fund*** works. When you begin investing, you must decide whether you want to pick individual stocks yourself or whether you want to hire someone else to compose a portfolio for you. A mutual fund holds shares of dozens, and often hundreds, of different companies.

Numerous investors pool their money together, and a fund manager invests this pool of money. The fund manager selects the stocks included in the fund. In exchange for his expertise, you pay him a fee. This fee is called an *expense ratio* and is a percentage of the overall assets you are investing in the fund. For example, if the fund has an expense ratio of 1 percent, expect to pay one dollar for every one hundred dollars you invest. Just as some chefs have higher rates but might not necessarily cook you a better meal, some mutual fund managers charge exorbitant fees but do not necessarily deliver above-average performance.

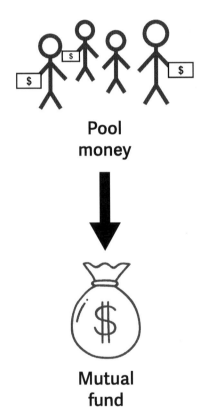

**Pool
money**

**Mutual
fund**

STOCK MARKET INDEXES

There are hundreds of thousands of publicly traded companies in the world. An index is a group of stocks that represents a specific part of the stock market. Some indexes provide a gauge of how well a segment of the market is performing, while others serve as an indicator of the overall market's performance. Indexes can be used as benchmarks to compare the performance of an individual stock, an exchange-traded fund (ETF), or a mutual fund to the overall market performance. Different indexes represent different parts of the market, and sector-specific indexes are a convenient way to measure the performance of certain types of companies.

There are three major indexes in the United States: The Dow Jones Industrial Average, the Nasdaq Composite, and the S&P 500.

	Dow Jones Industrial Average (the Dow)	Nasdaq Composite	S&P 500
Types of companies	Major, established, brand name companies	Tech	Large companies across most sectors
Examples of companies	Disney, Home Depot, Salesforce, Walmart	Netflix, Amazon, Apple, Nvidia, PayPal	Microsoft, Visa, Johnson & Johnson, JP Morgan Chase & Co, Tesla
Number of companies	30	Over 2,500	500

DOW JONES INDUSTRIAL AVERAGE (THE DOW)

The Dow Jones Industrial Average (commonly referred to as "the Dow") only included twelve companies, most of which were in the industrial sector, when it launched in 1896. At the time, the performance of industrial companies was closely associated with the health and growth of the economy. Today, the Dow tracks thirty large companies, most of which are household names that are considered influential in their respective industries. The composition of the index may shift as trends do to ensure that the Dow continues to provide a snapshot of broader market and economic activity, although, historically, the Dow's companies rarely change.

NASDAQ COMPOSITE INDEX

The Nasdaq Composite tracks companies listed on the Nasdaq stock exchange. Because the Nasdaq lists so many tech companies, the Nasdaq Composite Index is often viewed as a good measure of how well tech and growth companies are performing.

S&P 500

The Standard & Poor's 500 (S&P 500) consists of the five hundred largest publicly traded companies in the United States stock market. This index is often considered to be the best overall touchstone of how US stocks are performing. It has broader market exposure than the Dow. If the S&P 500 returned 11 percent one year and a company you invested in returned 4 percent, you might say your company underperformed the market.

PASSIVELY MANAGED VS. ACTIVELY MANAGED FUNDS

- **Passively Managed:** Passively managed funds mirror specific market indexes. Since the market historically keeps rising, the idea is your portfolio will grow along with it. No investment decisions need to be made. For example, an S&P 500 index fund simply consists of whichever companies are a part of the index. As fund managers do not have to make important decisions, passively managed funds generally have lower expense ratios than actively managed funds. This means you don't have to pay as much in fees.

- **Actively Managed:** Actively managed funds employ professionals, called fund managers, to research companies and to make decisions about when to buy, hold, and sell stocks. The fund manager's goal is to outperform benchmarks like the S&P 500. In other words, he wants to provide above-average returns for investors so that they will continue to pay him to manage their money. It is critical to consider fees when you are deciding how to invest your dollars. Though they can seem nominal, they can chip away at your returns over time. For instance, if you invest $5,000 in a fund with an expense ratio of 0.80 percent, you aren't just losing the forty dollars the fund manager pockets—you are also losing forty dollars that could have had the chance to compound and grow for years into the future.

EXCHANGE TRADED FUNDS (ETFS)

An *exchange-traded fund* (ETF) is a basket of assets. ETFs allow investors to own pieces of several companies with a single purchase. Often, they have specific focuses. For example, there are emerging market and cybersecurity ETFs. Many ETFs also track market indexes.

ETFs and mutual funds are quite similar in the sense that both allow you to spread your money around between a variety of investments. The main difference between the investment vehicles lies in how shares are traded. An ETF trades just like an individual stock; you can purchase and sell shares of an ETF at any given time during the trading day. Meanwhile, shares of traditional mutual funds can only be bought and sold once daily after the market closes.

INDEX FUNDS

You can own all the companies that are a part of a particular market index through investing in a fund that tracks it. An *index fund* is an ETF or mutual fund whose holdings mimic those of a particular market index. For example, the SPDR S&P 500 ETF tracks all five hundred companies in the S&P 500.

Fundamentally, a market index is a grouping of stocks. Imagine you walk into a large confectionary that just opened on the corner of town. The candy store has thousands of sweet treats available in a variety of flavors. An index fund that tracks a specific sector like retail could be compared to a box of assorted chocolates, while another sector-specific index fund could be compared to a bag of taffies. The S&P 500 index fund could be thought of as an assorted bag that contains a piece of the five hundred most popular candies in the store. Meanwhile, the Vanguard Total Market Index Fund, which is designed to mimic the performance of the entire US stock market, could be compared to a bag composed of a piece of every single sweet in the store—you get a taste of everything.

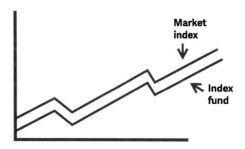

Warren Buffett is a staunch advocate of index funds. At Berkshire Hathaway's 2020 annual meeting, he claimed, "In my view, for most people, the best thing to do is to own the S&P 500 index fund." He even instructed the trustee who will be in charge of his estate to invest 90 percent of his money into "these assets" for his widow.[39]

Here's why index funds are such a great investment choice for many people:

1. **Average returns.** Although actively managed mutual funds employ professionals in an attempt to provide above-average returns for investors, many actively managed funds actually underperform the market. Index funds are passively managed and match the market's returns.
2. **Low costs.** In general, the average expense ratios for index funds are significantly lower than those of actively

---

39   Anna-Louise Jackson, "Warren Buffett: 'For Most People, the Best Thing' Is to Own This Kind of Index Fund," *Grow,* updated October 12, 2020.

managed funds. Even nominal fees can chip away at your returns very quickly. Not paying someone a sizable sum to pick and choose your investments means that you keep more money which you can reinvest in your portfolio. For example, as of this writing, the expense ratio of the SPDR S&P 500 ETF is 0.09 percent. Let's contrast your returns if you invested $10,000 in an index fund with a 0.09 percent expense ratio versus an actively managed fund with a 1 percent expense ratio, assuming a 7 percent annual rate of return. After forty-five years, your money in the index fund would grow to $202,220. After the same length of time, your money in the fund with the 1 percent ratio would only grow to $137,646. In other words, the total cost of choosing the more expensive fund would be $64,574. Investment costs add up, compounding along with your returns.

3. **Set it and forget it.** Index funds require little time or intelligence. Once you have made an initial investment, you don't have to worry about your money, besides regularly adding more!

4. **Diversification.** Buffett commented at his company's annual meeting, "With the exception of Berkshire, I would not want to put all my money in any one company. You get surprises in this world, and there will be businesses we think are very good that turn out not to be so good, and there will be other businesses that turn out better than we think."[40] When you are invested in an index fund, you don't have to hunt for the golden egg stocks to benefit from the market's overall gains. As your money is spread between numerous different companies, your

---

40 Ibid.

portfolio won't be endangered if a few don't do well. We will talk a bit more about diversification and its benefits in a later chapter, but this strategy can be thought of as "not keeping all your eggs in one basket." It is central to risk management and, concomitantly, successful investing.

You should research a fund you are interested in just as you would any other asset. Begin by asking yourself the following questions:

1. Which companies are being tracked by the fund?
Is the fund tracking the S&P 500? Financial technology companies? Artificial intelligence companies? Aerospace companies?

2. What fees am I paying?
What is the expense ratio on the fund? Is it reasonable?

Karen Finerman observes , "You don't have to understand stocks. Because of ETFs, it's a very reasonable position to just put your money in an S&P 500 ETF with Vanguard and leave it. You can buy a few different ETFs and get some US exposure, small-cap exposure, and worldwide exposure. Don't be afraid to invest because you don't know how to read an income statement or a balance sheet or don't know how the stock market works." Jennifer Barrett, chief education officer of Acorns, agrees, "When you're starting to invest, it's smart to put money into ETFs, like an S&P 500 index fund, so you are diversifying and trying to match the market with a good amount of your investment money versus trying to beat it. Then, you can invest a portion of your money in specific stocks and bonds, but I would caution against jumping right in and throwing your money into single stocks on the off chance you will pick one that does really well, as you are taking on a significantly higher degree of risk." Acorns, where Barrett works, offers pre-selected portfolios composed of funds with exposure to thousands of stocks and bonds.

***

Low-cost index funds are excellent options for rookie investors. They make it quick and easy to gain broad exposure to the market without paying exorbitant fees. If you have the psychological hurdle of "Personal finance and investing are complicated" or "I'm busy and don't have enough time," index funds may be perfect for you. Investing in an index fund involves near-zero effort and virtually no cost. Index funds may seem rather vanilla, but boring is often best when it comes to investing. If you stick with your investment over time, you are practically guaranteed to match the market's historical average return. As mentioned earlier, the overall stock market is expected to deliver a 7 percent annual real return over time. There is no simpler way to build wealth than by automating monthly investments into a low-cost S&P 500 index fund. Learning about and investing in individual stocks may afford you higher returns, but it also requires more time and practice than just investing in a fund. The rewards may be greater but so is the risk!

FUN FACTS

- There are a lot of peculiar ETFs, such as the Obesity ETF.
- The Dow Jones Industrial Average is the second oldest US stock market index.

Z NOTES

- A mutual fund pools the money of several investors to buy stocks, bonds, and other securities.
- An ETF is a basket of assets.
- The primary difference between mutual funds and ETFs is that ETFs trade just like stocks, so investors can purchase or sell shares at any given time during the trading day.
- Index funds track market indexes. They are a great investment option because they afford you average returns, do not charge hefty fees, do not require special skills or intelligence, and provide you with instant diversification.
- Pay attention to a fund's expense ratio and other fees. Though they may seem trivial, fees chip away at your returns over time.

CHAPTER 12

Do Your Homework: Evaluating Companies

———

"An investment in knowledge pays the best interest."

—BENJAMIN FRANKLIN

When shopping for a car, do you buy the first one you see at a dealership? Probably not. Shopping for a car is comparable to deciding which companies to invest in. Begin by thinking about your individual preferences and why you need the vehicle. It's important to consider whether you desire a ride that is fast and exciting but carries risk, such as a motorcycle, or whether you want a more conservative ride, such as a minivan. Similarly, when choosing individual companies, you have to consider whether you seek smaller, rapidly growing companies that carry more risk but also the potential for greater returns or whether you want to invest in brand-name, well-established companies that have a greater guarantee of returns. Then, just as you must research different car models with the intention of finding a vehicle that aligns with your needs and lifestyle at a suitable price, you must pick companies that will propel you toward your financial goals. Although it may feel a little daunting at first, learning how to pick individual stocks is important if you wish to try to beat the market's average historical return. Even if you don't wish to purchase stocks of individual companies, learning a few ways to evaluate them can help you gain a deeper understanding of the stock market. When choosing individual stocks, savvy shopping is the secret sauce to a profitable portfolio.

Luckily for Gen Z, information has never been more readily available. I recommend downloading an app such as CNBC's to help you keep track of companies you might be interested in investing in and to keep track of what's happening in the business world. CNBC's app provides you with a description of a given company, a list of its executives, its sector and industry, its website information, its market cap, its share price, and its P/E ratio, in addition to several other key business stats. It also lists germane articles in the news that involve the company. Don't worry if you aren't familiar with some of the terms I just listed, as we will explore them throughout this chapter. Before we begin building your evaluation toolkit, note that a tool called a stock screener can help you filter through investment choices according to size, price, sector, and other features.

If you have the psychological hurdle of "I'm not good at math," don't fear. Evaluating companies often comes down to common sense, a bit of research, and division.

When you purchase something, such as a pair of sneakers, what factors are involved in your decision-making process?

I'd imagine that you primarily focus on the quality and price of the product. Picking companies to invest in is no different. Determining whether a company is a wise investment boils down to quality and share price. Purchasing strong companies at attractive prices is the key to successfully selecting individual stocks. Use the following two questions as a basic framework for investment decisions:

- Is this a strong, well-run company with promising prospects?
- Is the stock reasonably priced or is it too expensive?

DETERMINING QUALITY AND PROSPECTS

COMPETITIVE ENVIRONMENT

Karen Finerman advises, "Look at qualitative metrics in addition to quantitative [metrics]. What is the brand? How competitive is the business? Is there any new technology that could make this business potentially obsolete? These are important things to understand." She adds, "Some companies are cheap for a reason. Blockbuster may have looked cheap two or three years before it went out of business."

Think about whether your company has any edge over its competition. Consumers want companies that suit their needs. Netflix demolished Blockbuster because its business model suited the entertainment needs of Americans better. It allowed people to stream movies and TV shows anytime, anywhere while only paying a few bucks per month. Blockbuster required its customers to trek to a physical Blockbuster location and charged many fees. When evaluating a company, note how the price and quality of the competition's products and services compare to those of the company you are interested in.

STRONG MANAGEMENT

Before you invest in a company, you need to ensure you believe in its management team. How much do you know about the CEO and other company executives? Does the CEO seem to be building a strong company that will thrive for years into the future or are they just seeking short-term profitability? Ideally, the CEO has a positive track record. It does not matter how unique and amazing a company's product or service is if the wrong people are making important decisions.

TRENDS

When determining which companies have favorable prospects, consider focusing on how the company taps into societal trends. For example, during the COVID-19 pandemic, companies that facilitated the digital transition grew and performed well.

UNDERSTANDING STOCK PRICES

Even the best companies can trade at prices higher than what they "deserve." Don't focus too much on the share price of a company itself. Comparing the share prices of different companies is meaningless because share price depends on the total number of shares available. For example, Apple has undergone multiple *stock splits*. A stock split decreases the numerical market price of individual shares but does not change the total value of a company because the total number of shares increases. Tiffany owns one share of Hannah's Honey at fifty dollars. The company undergoes a two-for-one stock split. Tiffany still owns fifty dollars total of Hannah's Honey, but she now has two twenty-five-dollar shares. To understand a company's stock price, you need context.

Valuation is the process of determining how much a company is worth. Through valuation, an investor aims to determine whether a company's shares are trading at a reasonable price.

MARKET CAP

Companies are often segmented by *market capitalization* (aka "market cap"). Market cap simply refers to the size of a company. To determine a company's market cap, multiply the total number of shares outstanding by the price per share. If a company has one thousand shares priced at $100 each, its market cap is $100,000 ($100 x one thousand shares).

Think of it like this: if you want to calculate the value of a bunch of bananas at the grocery store, simply multiply the price per banana by the number of bananas in the bunch. Similarly, if you want to calculate the market cap of a company, multiply its share price by the number of shares that exist. Market cap is the total value of a company. A company's market cap represents how highly the stock market is valuing it at a given time. It constantly shifts as its share price changes.

Size	Description
Small-Cap	Companies worth between $300 million and $2 billion
Medium-Cap	Companies worth between $2 billion and $10 billion
Large-Cap	Companies worth more than $10 billion

Companies in the same market cap category tend to share similar qualities. Large-caps are generally stable companies, while small-caps and mid-caps are not as well-established but tend to carry larger growth potential. The Russell 2000 index tracks small-cap companies, while the S&P 500 tracks US large-cap companies.

PRICE-TO-EARNINGS (P/E) RATIO

The *price-to-earnings ratio* is a useful metric for determining whether you are paying a fair price for a stock. A P/E ratio relates how highly the market is valuing a company to how much it actually earns. There are two main factors that determine a company's P/E ratio: share price and earnings per share (EPS). You already know what share price is, but what is earnings per share (EPS)? EPS is a company's net income divided by its total number of shares outstanding. A company's price-to-earnings ratio is its share price divided by its earnings per share.

$$P/E = \frac{\text{share price}}{\text{earnings per share (EPS)}}$$

Now that you have a basic understanding of what P/E ratios are, let's explore how they can help you determine whether a company's shares are reasonably priced. Imagine Company A and Company B both had one dollar in earnings per share last year. Company A is now trading at thirty dollars per share. Simply divide thirty by one to determine that Company A has a P/E ratio of thirty. Meanwhile, Company B is trading at twelve dollars per share. Divide twelve by one to determine that Company B has a P/E ratio of twelve. If both companies have the same earnings per share, why is Company A trading at thirty dollars while Company B is trading at twelve dollars?

Well, a company's P/E ratio often expresses investors' expectations of and the growth potential of that company. If a company has a high P/E ratio, it may mean investors have high growth expectations for that company or its stock is simply overvalued. Meanwhile, a low P/E ratio may signify that a company has a lower growth rate or is undervalued. The historical average P/E ratio is around fifteen. If a company is overvalued, you may be paying a high price for its stock relative to its intrinsic value. Meanwhile, if a company is undervalued, you could be getting a bargain because the company is trading at a low price relative to its intrinsic value. High-growth companies often have high P/E ratios because investors expect their earnings will increase in the foreseeable future. For example, in 2020, fintech company Square had a P/E ratio of over seven hundred because investors expected it would continue to innovate and grow. The average P/E varies across sectors (see below), so it can be helpful to compare a company's P/E ratio to the average P/E ratio of the sector to which it belongs.

Note that sometimes what appears to be a "cheap" stock may actually be cheap because it has a poor business model and low potential for future growth. This type of company may be considered a "value trap." As Finerman explained, this is where factoring in a company's quality and inspecting non-financial metrics can be helpful.

PRICE-EARNINGS-GROWTH (PEG) RATIO

If a company with a thirty P/E has a higher growth rate than a company with a twelve P/E, the company with the higher ratio may actually be more fairly priced. This is where the *price-earnings-growth ratio* can be helpful. The PEG ratio allows you to determine whether a company is overvalued or undervalued in the context of its growth rate. Investors profit through price appreciation of the shares of stock they own. Therefore, investors want to own companies that will increase in value over time. Purchasing companies at attractive prices that have the potential to grow and increase in value is the key to profit. Calculating a company's PEG ratio is straightforward. Divide its P/E ratio by its expected earnings growth rate.

$$\text{PEG ratio} = \frac{\text{price to earnings ratio}}{\text{earnings growth rate}}$$

Imagine Cassie's Clay Masks is expected to grow 20 percent in the coming year. The company has a P/E ratio of fifteen. The company's PEG ratio is 0.75 (15/20 = 0.75). In general, a PEG ratio of less than one is considered to be indicative of an undervalued stock, while a PEG ratio of more than one is considered to be indicative of an overvalued stock.

REVENUE

Revenue is the income a business generates from its sales of goods and services to customers. Quarterly or annual increases in a company's revenue may indicate it is growing.

PRICE-TO-SALES (P/S) RATIO

The price-to-sales ratio is an especially handy tool for evaluating unprofitable companies because the metric is based on revenue. If a company's earnings are negative, calculating its P/E ratio is not useful because the denominator of the equation is less than zero. Some investors understand certain companies need to spend and reinvest their cash in order to grow. The P/S ratio relates a company's stock price to its sales. To calculate a company's P/S ratio, divide its market cap by its revenue.

$$P/S = \frac{\text{market cap}}{\text{revenue}}$$

If a company had a P/S ratio of two, it would mean that investors were willing to pay two dollars per share for every dollar of the company's sales. In general, the lower the P/S ratio, the better, as you are paying less for each dollar of a company's sales.

CATEGORIZATIONS

Every company is different. Many companies are categorized according to their specific characteristics. We've already taken a look at size (market cap). While numbers are certainly an important part of evaluating potential companies to invest in, understanding the categories to which a company belongs can give you some important information about it. Let's go through a few common stock categorizations.

SECTORS

The term *sector* is used to describe a specific segment of the economy. Each sector encompasses companies that share similar characteristics in terms of the goods they sell or the services they provide. There are eleven stock market sectors, as outlined by the Global Industry Classification Standard (GICS):

- Communication services
- Consumer discretionary
- Consumer staples
- Energy
- Financials
- Healthcare
- Industrials
- Materials
- Real estate
- Technology
- Utilities

For example, the technology sector encompasses the likes of Apple, Google, Amazon, Facebook, Microsoft, and Netflix.

Understanding the sectors to which different companies belong can help you compare limes to lemons, not apples to oranges, when using ratios as metrics to appraise stocks. Typical P/E and PEG ratios tend to vary between sectors. You don't necessarily want to compare Nvidia to McDonald's. Good examples of comparisons might be Apple to Microsoft or JP Morgan to Bank of America.

BLUE CHIP STOCKS AND PENNY STOCKS

Some classifications indicate a company's quality. Blue chip stocks are reputable, industry-leading, large-cap companies. Although they generally do not generate very high returns, blue chip stocks offer investors with an option for lower risk stability.

On the other hand, penny stocks are inexpensive. Despite their name, penny stocks seldom cost a mere penny. Penny stocks trade for less than five dollars. They can be *very* speculative and fluctuate dramatically in share price. With the extreme volatility, why would people want to take a risk and invest in penny stocks? Simply put, because penny stocks tend to be volatile, many people think they can capitalize on penny stocks' price swings and make a few quick bucks. It is generally accepted that investing in penny stocks is not judicious for a beginner who is taking a long-term approach to investing, as the downside associated with these investments can be profound.

GROWTH STOCKS AND VALUE STOCKS

Growth investing and value investing are both common investing techniques. Value investors pursue companies whose share prices are low compared to their intrinsic value, while growth investors seek companies experiencing rapid increases in revenue and profits.

Value stocks are generally regarded as safe investments. They are often brand-name companies and are generally good options for investors seeking stability. Growth stocks are associated with a relatively high degree of risk, but their potential returns can also be sizable. Successful growth companies align with societal trends.

STICK WITH WHAT YOU KNOW

Peter Lynch is a famous mutual fund manager. During his tenure as manager of the Fidelity Magellan Fund, he consistently beat the market's average return by a large margin. In his book *One Up on Wall Street,* Lynch maintains that the average investor can be more successful than the pros when they leverage what they know. The acquisition of deep knowledge in a particular area often translates to the ability to make educated guesses about which companies will perform well in that domain. Investing is an opportunity to build your wealth through owning pieces of the businesses you love. Consider investing in what you know or in what interests you. If you are a self-proclaimed tech nerd, you can invest in tech companies. If you can be found in your garden on Saturday mornings, perhaps a company like Home Depot is a good investment for you.

Discuss your ideas with friends and family. Community is an important aspect of successful investing. Everyone has different interests. For example, if you have one friend interested in artificial intelligence and another knowledgeable in the realm of e-commerce, then you can expand your horizons and become well-informed in those domains, too.

CONSIDER BUILDING A MOCK PORTFOLIO

Before plunking your hard-earned dollars into the real stock market, it can be wise to set up a mock portfolio. Several brokerages and financial websites offer simulated investing platforms. Setting up a mock portfolio can be a smart move before investing in individual stocks for a few reasons. For one, it allows you to familiarize yourself with the mechanics of the stock market. You will learn how the market reacts to global events and will see the daily fluctuations in stock prices. A mock portfolio also allows you to test out new investment strategies without risking your own money. Many stock market simulators give users virtual cash. You may consider using TD Ameritrade's paperMoney Virtual Stock Market Simulator or Fidelity's Wealthbase.

CREATE A WATCH LIST

A *watch list* helps you keep track of companies in which you are interested in investing. Add companies that you like to your watch list. Then, track their performance by following price moves and news related to them (e.g., new products, initiatives, etc.). CNBC's app offers an option to build a watch list.

KNOW WHY YOU ARE BUYING

After you research companies and choose to invest in them, ensure you have clear rationale. You should always know *why* you are making a particular investment. Did the company just introduce a new product you feel will sell well and result in profits? Did you do the math and find the company is attractively priced with high growth potential? Before pulling the trigger on the investment, record your logic in a small investment notebook or journal.

***

There is no single correct way to analyze individual stocks and investing decisions should not be made based on a single metric, so it is important to build your toolkit. Also, keep in mind there is no one-size-fits-all approach to investing. You can invest in both small-cap and large-cap companies. You can own both growth and value stocks. If picking individual stocks seems intimidating, remember that they are not the only way to grow your money. You can invest in mutual funds or exchange traded funds (ETFs), which allow you to own pieces of multiple companies at once. Investing in these "baskets of stocks" automatically diversifies your portfolio and is less risky than investing in individual companies—a concept that will be explored in depth in Chapter 14. You may consider keeping the majority of your money in an index fund and investing in five to fifteen individual companies. Investing is an opportunity to build your wealth through owning pieces of the businesses you love.

FUN FACTS
- The first company to achieve a market capitalization of $2 trillion was Apple.
- The label "blue chip" comes from the game of poker in which blue chips typically have the highest values.

Z NOTES

- Research a company before you purchase its stock.
- Don't buy a stock based on a hot tip or because you heard someone else bragging about it. Buy a stock congruent with your interests and that you have evaluated with several metrics.
- You can become a successful investor by purchasing quality companies at reasonable prices.
- There is no perfect way to pick stocks, so develop your own evaluation toolkit.
- Solid analysis can help you make informed decisions. The goal of stock analysis is to pick companies you believe have good values and favorable long-term prospects. Keep your emotions out of your decision making!
- Before you invest in a company, ensure you understand what you are buying and *why*; you should have clear reasons.

CHAPTER 13

Financing Your Future

———

"My parents didn't want to move to Florida, but they turned sixty and that's the law."

—JERRY SEINFELD

"What do you want to be when you grow up?" Ah, this classic question, posed to so many youngsters, often results in one of two responses: an awkward laugh or a passionate description of a dream job. It can be hard to think about the future, let alone retiring. It's tempting to tell yourself you will begin saving and investing when your earnings increase, but when it comes to saving for retirement, the earlier you begin, the more flexibility you will have to create the future you envision for yourself. Small amounts of money can multiply to large sums when they have time to grow with compound interest.

Remember the story of Janet and Ted from the "Growing Your Own Money Tree" chapter? Let's go over it again to ensure you remember the power of time.

Janet and Ted are twenty-year-old twins, and they both aim to retire when they are sixty-five years old. Janet and Ted make a bet one day about who will have a larger nest egg come retirement. Janet invests $1,000 per year until she is thirty-five and then stops saving for retirement and contributing to her investments. In total, she invests $15,000. Meanwhile, Ted begins investing when he is thirty-five and invests $1,000 per year until he turns sixty-five. In total, he invests $30,000.

Ted invests twice as much as Janet. Both Janet and Ted earn the stock market's average annual 7 percent real return. When retirement arrives, who has a larger nest egg, Janet or Ted? It's Janet. Janet has $219,006 to show for Ted's $101,073.

Even though Janet only invested half the sum Ted did, when it comes time to retire, her nest egg is more than double the size of Ted's because she began investing fifteen years earlier. The moral of the story: do not wait to invest in yourself. Because of compound growth, the sooner you begin investing for retirement, the less money you will need to save to end up with the same amount that you need to retire.

In this chapter, we will explore some of the most common vehicles you can use to save for retirement and big life milestones. Although this isn't the most entertaining reading, lounging on a beach in Greece sipping a drink with a mini umbrella sounds fun, no? Yeah, that's what I thought. Investing in yourself early will help you enjoy that beach a lot more.

INDIVIDUAL RETIREMENT ACCOUNTS (IRAS)

IRAs are tax-advantaged accounts that enable individuals to save and invest money for retirement. To open an IRA, you must earn income. If you are younger than eighteen, you can still open an IRA, but your parent or legal guardian must serve as a custodian (we will explore custodial accounts in greater depth in Chapter 14). There are two main types of IRAs: *traditional IRAs* and *Roth IRAs.*

You invest *pretax* money in a traditional IRA—your income is not taxed before it is invested in the IRA. You pay taxes when you withdraw the money.

Meanwhile, you invest *post-tax* money in a Roth IRA and never have to pay taxes on your money in the account. Opening a Roth IRA is like planting a grove of apple trees. Each tree represents an investment. The earlier you plant the trees, the more time they have to grow. Today, you purchase the seeds. Over the course of several years, you monitor the trees to ensure they are developing optimally. When retirement arrives, some of your trees will be strong, fruitful, and have produced delicious apples. At that point, you can just sit back and take a big bite.

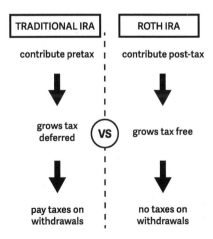

Tax-advantaged retirement accounts have stringent specifications on when and how you can withdraw money from them. You can withdraw contributions you make to a Roth IRA anytime without having to pay taxes or penalties. However, if you withdraw earnings from the account before age fifty-nine-and-a-half or before the account has been open for at least five years, you have to pay taxes and an early withdrawal penalty (you are exempt from this rule in certain situations like buying your first home). Contributions are the money you directly invest in the account, while earnings are the dollars generated from your investments in the account. For example, if you contributed $4,000 to a Roth IRA and your money has grown to $6,000 a few years later, you can withdraw the $4,000 penalty-free, if you wish. Withdrawals from a traditional IRA before age fifty-nine-and-a-half are taxed and penalized 10 percent. These restrictions are Uncle Sam's way of ensuring you don't blow all your retirement savings on a fancy car.

The government also limits the sum you can contribute to your tax-advantaged retirement accounts each year. In 2021, the annual contribution limit for an IRA was $6,000 for those under the age of fifty and $7,000 for those age fifty and older. Income and contribution limits can vary from year to year so be sure to check the current amounts.

IS A ROTH IRA OR A TRADITIONAL IRA BETTER?

Generally speaking, Roth IRAs provide distinctly beneficial tax advantages for young people. Assuming you don't tap your IRA early, your final account balance should exceed the sum you contribute. Recall that you pay taxes upfront on your Roth IRA contributions. You must pay taxes on both your contributions and earnings generated in a traditional IRA. Plus, because you are young, you may be in a lower tax bracket now than you will be when you are older. To put it all together, you are likely paying taxes on less money and at a lower rate with a Roth IRA. Therefore, your tax burden is significantly lower with a Roth IRA than with a traditional IRA, making it an excellent investment vehicle for Gen Z.

401(K)S

401(k)s are similar to IRAs in that they are tax-advantaged retirement accounts. However, the biggest distinction between the retirement vehicles is that 401(k)s are employer sponsored.

The majority of employers used to offer pension funds through which employees would receive a steady stream of income over the course of their retirement. However, as running pensions became increasingly expensive, employers began to offer employees 401(k)s, which transfer the responsibility of investing for retirement to employees and allow employees to control how their money is invested.

Your employer may contribute a certain amount to your 401(k) based on how much you contribute. These contributions are called employer matches. Imagine your employer offered its employees a match up to 3 percent. If you contributed 3 percent of your $60,000 salary ($1,800) to your 401(k), your company would also contribute $1,800. Although you could add more than the $1,800, your company would only match up to 3 percent. You should *always* strive to take full advantage of your employer match. If you don't, you are essentially leaving free money on the table which, thanks to compounding, could grow to a tremendous sum.

Your employer may offer both traditional 401(k)s and Roth 401(k)s. The differences between the two are very similar to the differences between traditional IRAs and Roth IRAs. While a traditional 401(k) is tax-deferred, meaning you pay taxes on your funds upon withdrawal, you pay taxes on Roth 401(k) contributions upfront.

Note that, just like with IRAs, the government imposes limits on when you can withdraw funds from your 401(k) and sets contribution limits. If you withdraw early, you will be taxed and charged a 10 percent penalty. In 2020, the contribution limit for employees participating in a 401(k) was $19,500. Just like with IRAs, contribution limits can change from year to year.

Keep in mind you can contribute to an IRA and a 401(k) simultaneously. I recommend taking advantage of these tax-advantaged accounts as much as you can. The more you save in taxes, the more money you can invest for your future!

SOCIAL SECURITY
Signed into law by Franklin D. Roosevelt in 1935, Social Security is a federal program that provides money to Americans that are of retirement age, disabled, or a survivor of a deceased worker. Here's how it works: When you are a baby, you receive a Social Security number. This number becomes important when you begin working. When you get your first

job, you begin paying FICA (i.e., payroll) taxes, which fund Social Security. Adults pay into Social Security during their working years with the expectation that they will receive benefits themselves down the road. Today's workers are funding the benefits for today's recipients.

Social Security is controversial; it is anticipated that there will eventually be more people collecting benefits than paying into the program. It is estimated that Social Security's trust funds will be depleted by 2035, in which case only around 80 percent of promised benefits would be payable. Zoomers cannot rely on Social Security benefits or pension funds, making it critical we begin saving and investing for retirement as early as possible.

529 SAVINGS PLANS

Run at the state level, 529 savings plans are tax-advantaged college savings accounts. They allow an account holder to contribute funds that grow tax free (kind of like a retirement account but for education expenses). The account holder can withdraw the funds in the account without paying taxes on them given they are being used for qualified higher education expenses or for elementary/secondary school tuition for the designated beneficiary. Qualified college expenses are quite broad and include room and board, textbooks, and tuition.

∗∗∗

Although retirement may seem ages away, it is wise to begin planning *now*. If you are a high school student or college student reading this book, you may already have a part-time or summer job. If you are not contributing to an IRA, look into it or chat with a trusted adult about it. When I was fourteen, I worked my first job cleaning dental instruments in a dental office. As soon as I received my first paycheck, I invested all the money into a Roth IRA. My money has already grown, and every time I earn more, I always invest it in my Roth IRA because I know over time it will grow and help fund a cushy retirement.

Self-care is trendy. For some people, it might look like doing a sheet mask or journaling. While investing in your future might not seem like the most conventional or trendy form of self-care, it is very effective and will pay dividends for years to come.

FUN FACTS

- The Social Security Administration uses Social Security applications to develop an annual list of the ten most popular baby names. In 2019, Liam and Olivia topped the list.
- Elderly people don't just move to Florida for the warm, sunny weather. Florida also has no state income tax.
- Proponents of the FIRE (Financial Independence Retire Early) movement save aggressively and live frugally in an effort to retire years or even decades earlier than they would otherwise be able to.

Z NOTES

- IRAs and 401(k)s are the two main types of retirement investing vehicles. The main difference is that 401(k)s are sponsored by an employer, while you can set up an IRA on your own, given you earn income.
- The biggest distinction between retirement accounts is whether your contributions are made on a pre-tax or post-tax basis.
- If you are young and expect to be in a higher tax bracket than you are now when you withdraw your funds, investing in a Roth IRA is a great choice for you. Investing in a Roth IRA means your money can grow with the power of compound interest tax-free.
- The government imposes limits on how and when you can withdraw from tax-advantaged retirement accounts.

- A 529 savings plan is a tax-advantaged education investment account. An account holder can withdraw the funds in the account without paying taxes on them given they are going toward qualified higher education expenses or elementary/secondary school tuition for the designated beneficiary.
- It pays to begin investing in your future now. Every bit of money you can save and invest will help you down the road. Consider automating your IRA and/or 401(k) contributions.

CHAPTER 14

Getting Started

—

"Everyone has the brainpower to follow the stock market. If you made it through fifth-grade math, you can do it."

-PETER LYNCH

Imagine you were handed $500 to invest. What would you do first? Don't worry if you don't know. That's what this chapter is for. Before I walk you through how to begin putting your money into the stock market, though, there are a few crucial things you need to learn about. Let's dive right in.

YOUR RISK PROFILE

First thing's first: you need to determine your *time horizon.* In other words, you need to think about when you are actually going to need the money you plan to invest. Your time horizon is tied to the degree of risk associated with your investments. If you are sixteen years old and need your money for college tuition in two years, you have a short-time horizon and should have the money you will need stashed in a low-risk investment or bank account. Meanwhile, if you are in your twenties and saving for retirement, you have a long-time horizon and can likely afford to take more of an aggressive approach to investing.

Let's discuss risk a bit more. You likely take risks every day by procrastinating homework, trying to win an argument with your mom, or driving a car. The concept of risk is probably something you are quite familiar with in your personal life, but it also plays a role in financial decisions. *Risk tolerance* refers to the extent to which you are comfortable with the prospect of losing money on an investment and to which you are able to deal with volatility.

Let's look at an example to explore this concept. Donna and Lauren are best friends. They have a lot in common, but they have very different risk tolerances. Donna is uncomfortable with making risky investments; she has a low risk tolerance, meaning she is risk averse. She prefers being conservative with her money and has stashed half of it in a savings account and the other half in bonds. Even though Donna sacrifices high returns, she sleeps better at night knowing exactly where her money is. Meanwhile, Lauren is the opposite of Donna. As she has a high-risk tolerance, she invests the majority of her money in stocks. Imagine Donna and Lauren are both offered the chance to invest $1,000 for a guaranteed profit of $150. They are also offered the alternative of investing the same amount of money for a 60 percent chance of earning a $300 profit. Donna would most likely choose the $150 because she has a low risk appetite, while Lauren would probably opt for the $300 as she doesn't mind taking on a greater degree of risk for a larger potential return.

BUILDING YOUR PORTFOLIO

When you begin investing, you have a myriad of choices. You will curate a mixture of investments called a ***portfolio***. In developing your portfolio, you will go through a process called ***asset allocation***. This process simply entails deciding the ***asset classes*** in which you would like to invest and the portion of your portfolio that should be dedicated to each. Asset classes are groupings of similar types of investments. These are analogous to food groups. For example, kale, romaine, brussels sprout, cauliflower, and carrots are all vegetables. Vegetables are the "asset class." Equities (stocks), cash and cash equivalents (includes money kept in bank accounts), bonds, and alternative investments (real estate, art, cryptocurrency, etc.) are the main asset classes. If you have $1,000 and half of it is sitting in cash and the other half is invested in an S&P 500 index fund, you have a 50/50 allocation to cash and equities. Your time horizon, risk tolerance, and goals are the major factors determining this balance.

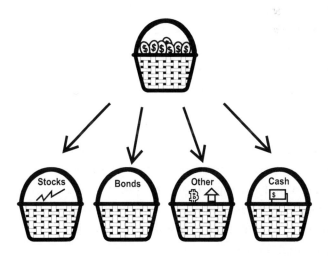

Many brokerages and robo-advisors offer prebuilt portfolios with labels such as "conservative," "moderate," and "aggressive." These labels reflect both time horizon and risk tolerance.

Conversative portfolios consist of low-risk investments that have relatively low potential for financial gains. They are generally intended for investors who need money in the short term. Aggressive portfolios are typically meant for investors who are willing to take on more risk to potentially earn more profit and who have a long-time horizon, as short-term market volatility won't inhibit their ability to reach their goals. As you may have guessed, moderate portfolios fall in between aggressive and conservative in terms of risk and potential for financial reward.

Think back to the risk pyramid in Chapter 10. If you have a long-time horizon, your portfolio may contain a high proportion of stocks, as you have time to ride out the market's ups and downs before you need your dollars. If you need money in the immediate future, your portfolio may contain a greater proportion of assets that carry less risk, such as cash. Low-risk investments shield you against short-term volatility in the market and ensure your money is available when you need it.

It is important to strike a balance when it comes to risk. It's not wise to have 80 percent of your portfolio in cryptocurrencies and the other 20 percent in stocks. Of course, you don't want to have a 100 percent allocation to cash, either, in which case you will automatically be losing money to inflation. It is important to give your money the chance to grow, but it is also important to not take on a degree of risk significantly higher than that with which you are comfortable, as doing so could result in panic selling at a bad time. The most effective way to balance your risk within your portfolio is to diversify. **Diversification** is crucial for minimizing your risk and ensuring your portfolio is not imperiled by a single bad investment. Karen Finerman, cofounder and CEO of Metropolitan Capital, states, "Having all your eggs in one basket is an elementary mistake."

"The biggest mistakes I see young investors making is over allocating in one trade," says JJ Kinahan, chief market strategist at TD Ameritrade. Thinking in partials and not 'all in, all out' is absolutely the biggest thing I think people have to think about. The fact we are at zero commissions now on equities really helps because it isn't cost prohibitive to think that way."

Diversification is closely tied to asset allocation. Just because you keep, say, 85 percent of your money in stocks does not mean that you should only invest in two or three companies. If a company tanks, you don't want to go down with it. As mentioned in previous chapters, holding shares of mutual funds, ETFs, and index funds provides you with instant diversification. To create a diversified portfolio, begin by spreading your investments around by asset class. Ensure that you have a small portion of your portfolio dedicated to cash, as it is imperative to have an emergency fund. Then, you can diversify within an asset class. For example, if you allocate 75 percent of your portfolio to equities, you could invest a portion of that money in an index fund and the other part in individual stocks. You could invest the money dedicated to individual stocks in companies of different sizes and in various sectors. Recall that different stocks have different degrees of risk associated with them. For example, growth stocks generally carry more risk than blue chip stocks.

Think about diversification like your diet. My guess is you don't just eat ice cream or chocolate, as your body would lack the key nutrients it needs to thrive. In the same way, your body would not function optimally if you just ate spinach and squash, no matter how good they seem for you. You probably know that the more variety of colors and nutrients you have on your plate, the better off you will be. Instead of just eating one food or food group, it is necessary to balance your plate with a variety of fruits, vegetables, dairy, protein, and complex carbohydrates. Your portfolio is similar; asset allocation is like building a dinner plate and diversification is ensuring that it is well-balanced. To manage your risk, you must diversify your investments.

"When I was in my late twenties, I worked at a company in Silicon Valley. I had more than $1 million in stock and stock options concentrated in the company. I had no idea what diversification meant, and I had no idea what asset allocation was. When the big tech bubble burst, I lost all of that in a matter of hours. I remember staring at my computer screen, looking at my brokerage account, watching the value plummet, and thinking I was in an alternate universe. It was devastating to watch myself lose that much money and to think it could have been preventable. It is interesting because, while I retained two homes, some of my colleagues literally lost everything. They were highly leveraged; they had leveraged their stock to buy a lot of other things, like multimillion dollar homes and fancy sports cars. Because they had borrowed against that stock, they had to repay the money they had borrowed by selling their assets, including assets they had come to the company with such as a house their mother had passed down to them. Diversification is extremely important."

—TANYA VAN COURT, FOUNDER OF GOALSETTER

Think of building your portfolio like baking a cake. Your ingredients are stocks, bonds, cash, and alternative investments. The amount of each kind of ingredient is similar to asset allocation, and the time in the oven is your time horizon.

BROKERAGES

By this point, if you have developed an emergency fund and don't have any high-interest debt, you may be ready to begin investing in the stock market. Congratulations! Again, you should not invest money you will need within the next couple of years in stocks, as the market can be volatile.

First, you need to decide how much you would like to invest. Revisit the cash flow plan you developed in Chapter 4. Recall that disposable income is your basic living expenses (rent, utilities, groceries) subtracted from your after-tax income. You can choose how much of your disposable income you wish to invest. After you do so, it's time to open a brokerage account.

I introduced you to brokerages in Chapter 10. Here is a refresher: A brokerage firm is a company that buys and sells securities on your behalf. Charles Schwab, Vanguard, Fidelity, E*Trade, and TD Ameritrade are all brokerages. Some brokerages only operate online, while others also have brick and mortar locations. Keep in mind there are now many companies whose missions are to democratize investing for rookies, like Acorns and Public, with whom you can invest in lieu of traditional brokerages (investing apps will be explored in greater depth in Chapter 17).

There are multiple types of investment accounts that you can open with a brokerage. Selecting the right account type depends on your answer to the question, "Why am I investing?" Are you investing for retirement, investing for education expenses, or simply looking to grow your money? If you are investing for retirement, consider opening an IRA. If you are investing for education costs, consider a 529 account. If you are investing for other goals, a standard brokerage account is the way to go. Note that you can invest in multiple types of accounts at once. It is generally recommended you take full advantage of tax-advantaged accounts.

You can invest if you are younger than eighteen, but you need adult sponsorship to open a brokerage account. Your mother, father, grandparents, or legal guardian can help you open a *custodial account.*

In general, there are three simple steps to follow when selecting a brokerage firm and opening an account:

1. Do your homework and comparison shop. Read up on a few different brokerage firms. You can utilize a website like Nerdwallet, which provides in-depth reviews of brokerages and financial products, to make an informed decision.
2. Find a brokerage you like and fill out an application.
3. Deposit money into your account.
4. Select your investments.

Let's say you want to purchase one share of Company X for fifty dollars. Deposit fifty dollars in your brokerage account and place the trade. It's that simple.

DIVIDEND REINVESTMENT PLANS (DRIPS)

A dividend reinvestment plan (DRIP) allows investors to deploy the dividends they receive from a company to buy additional fractional shares or whole shares of that company automatically. Let's say you own one seventy-dollar share of Company Y. Company Y pays a one-dollar dividend per share. As you participate in a DRIP, that one dollar is reinvested to purchase a fractional share of Company Y. Most brokerages offer DRIPs. Some companies offer them directly to their shareholders. Reinvesting your dividends allows you to put more money to work for you and can help your portfolio grow over time.

CAPITAL GAINS

When you invest in stocks, your shares may appreciate in value. Those profits are called ***capital gains***. When you sell your investments, Uncle Sam taxes your capital gains (profits). You don't have to pay taxes on capital gains until the gain is realized. In other words, you don't owe taxes on an investment until you sell it. For instance, if you own shares of Microsoft and the value of your shares increases every year, you do not have to pay any taxes until you sell the shares for more than you bought them.

There are two different types of capital gains:

1. Short-term capital gains: profits from investments owned for less than one year
2. Long-term capital gains: profits from investments owned for over one year

Short-term capital gains are taxed at the same rate as your federal income tax bracket. Long-term capital gains are either not taxed or are taxed at a rate significantly lower than that of your current tax bracket. (To clarify, based on your income, you are placed in a particular tax bracket. Refer to the "Adulting" chapter in Part 2 for a refresher, if necessary.) These hefty, short-term capital gains taxes are part of the reason why frequently trading stocks is not necessarily a profitable strategy, as you have to make quite a bit of profit to offset the taxes you must pay.

ROBO-ADVISORS

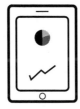 

Have you ever dreamed about a robot doing the dishes or going to school for you? If you have, you probably resonate with the concept of a *robo-advisor.* The popularity of robo-advisors has surged since they first emerged in the wake of the Great Recession. They align with the needs of young people, who have historically been excluded from the world of investing, and can serve as a great way for our digitally native generation to begin investing.

WHAT IS A ROBO-ADVISOR?

The term "robo-advisor" is misleading; robo-advisors are not robots. Rather, they are online services that utilize advanced algorithms to create and manage investment portfolios in an automated manner. Robo-advisors function similarly to Spotify. Just as Spotify generates song recommendations based on your personal preferences, robo-advisors use your data to recommend a pre-built portfolio.

When setting up a robo-advisor account, you complete a questionnaire that asks you about your age, time horizon, risk tolerance, and personal goals. Based on that information, the robo-advisor recommends a portfolio of funds that aligns with your preferences and goals. Typically, your dollars will be invested in ETFs from several brokerages. Once you deposit funds to be invested, the robo-advisor monitors your portfolio over time to ensure your investments are conducive to achieving your goals. Some robo-advisors allow you to speak with a CFP® or a financial professional if you request. After you've established your account and chosen a portfolio, you can track your progress and add contributions.

THE PROS AND CONS OF ROBO-ADVISORS

PROS

1. **Low Costs**

Traditional financial advisors charge hefty fees and require high minimum account balances to use their services. Robo-advisors are affordable. Most require minimum account balances of $500 or less, whereas many traditional financial advisors require large minimums (e.g., upwards of $20,000). Additionally, many robo-advisors charge a 0.25 percent account management fee or less, whereas many traditional advisors charge a fee in the ballpark of 0.5 percent to 2.5 percent of your assets. Paying lower fees means that you have more money in your pocket to invest.

2. **Automation of Complex Activities**
- **Tax-loss harvesting:** If you sell an investment for a profit, you owe taxes on your capital gains. However, selling investments for a loss can offset the capital gains taxes you owe on investments that have appreciated in value. In a nutshell, tax-loss harvesting is strategically selling investments that have dropped in price to reduce the amount of taxes you have to pay. Here's where it gets a

bit involved, though. You still want to have your money working for you in the market because, as long as you invest in strong companies, your investments will likely increase in value over time. Thus, when you sell an investment, you should purchase a similar investment. Most busy everyday investors simply don't have the time or enthusiasm to comb their portfolios for tax-loss harvesting possibilities, which is why this practice is one of the biggest benefits of utilizing a robo-advisor.

- **Rebalancing:** Rebalancing is the process of realigning the investments in your portfolio to match your desired asset allocation. Imagine you had a $20,000 portfolio with an 80 percent allocation to stocks and a 20 percent allocation to bonds. Your stocks delivered high returns for a few years, so the $16,000 you invested in stocks grew to $25,000. The $4,000 investment in bonds grew to $5,000. You now have an 83/17 allocation to stocks and bonds, respectively. You want to rebalance to get it back to the 80/20 sweet spot. Robo-advisors automatically rebalance your portfolio for you.

3. **A Steady Hand During Turbulent Times**
   As the name indicates, a robo-advisor removes your emotions from the picture.

CONS

1. **Limited customization:** A robo-advisor doesn't afford you the same level of portfolio individualization as a human financial advisor does. While a robo-advisor may be a good option for you if your needs are fairly simple, a human advisor may be better if your needs are complicated.

WHERE CAN I FIND A ROBO-ADVISOR?

Many large brokerage firms, including Schwab, Vanguard, and Fidelity, offer robo-advising services. Other robo-advisors to research include:

- Betterment
- Wealthfront
- Wealthsimple

Some robo-advising services affiliated with brokerages only invest in the firm's mutual funds and ETFs, which is a factor to consider when selecting a robo-advisor. Of course, that doesn't mean using a robo-advising tool offered by a brokerage is a bad option. Do your research to make an informed decision that suits your personal needs.

Andy Rachleff, cofounder and CEO of Wealthfront, remarks, "Because robo-advisors are inexpensive, fully digital, and easy to use, they are a great way for Gen Z to start investing. Unlike me (a Baby Boomer), today's younger investors are accustomed to doing everything right from an app, whether that's ordering food or finding a rideshare, so of course they expect to manage their money the same way. Plus, a robo-advisor offers [numerous] benefits through software, so you don't have to worry about picking stocks, doing manual trades, rebalancing, or executing tax-loss harvesting. We believe quality banking and investing services that are integrated with automation can be the greatest wealth creation engine this generation has ever seen, and we're excited for Gen Z to take advantage of that opportunity."

***

When it comes to beginning your investing journey, you have a lot of options. Begin by thinking about your personal goals and why investing is important to you. Your goals provide a framework for your overall approach to investing. Then, consider your individual time horizon and risk tolerance, which determine your asset allocation. You get to decide how hands-on you want to be when it comes to your portfolio. If the financial markets fascinate you, then you can take more of a DIY approach to investing. If you want to grow your money but don't want to worry about picking investments and following the market, then a robo-advisor may be advantageous to you. Your approach to investing will likely shift over time. However, one thing will remain the same: it is uniquely yours.

FUN FACTS
- Launched in 2008, Betterment was the first robo-advisor.
- Several robo-advisors are based on Nobel Prize-winning algorithms and models.

Z NOTES
- Your objectives inform everything from the types of brokerage accounts you should open to the investments you purchase.
- Your asset allocation is a function of your risk tolerance and time horizon.

- Diversification entails spreading your money across different investments. This strategy is essential for reducing risk.
- Before you begin investing, you should have an emergency fund established and high-interest debt paid off.
- A brokerage firm buys and sells securities on your behalf.
- Robo-advisors are online services that use advanced algorithms to manage and build investment portfolios automatically. They provide an efficient, low-cost solution to individuals beginning their investment journeys.
- Profits generated by your investments are called capital gains. When you sell your investments for a profit, your capital gains are subject to federal taxes. There are two types: short-term and long-term capital gains. Long-term capital gains are taxed at a significantly lower rate than short-term capital gains.

CHAPTER 15

The Bulls and the Bears

———

"Unless you can watch your stock holding decline by 50 percent without becoming panic-stricken, you should not be in the stock market."

—WARREN BUFFETT

The stock market *will* crash, dip, bump, plummet, plunge, trip, tumble, slide, dive, and drop during your time as an investor. Perhaps you have already invested during a financial downturn; many young investors began their journeys during the March 2020 stock market crash triggered by the COVID-19 pandemic.

Although there is no crystal ball to predict when the next major market decline will occur, learning about past downturns can help you thrive during the next one. Why? History has shown that the market rebounds after every crash and that investors who stick to their guns during tough periods are handsomely rewarded. Learning about past crashes and subsequent periods of prosperity can help you understand the cycles of the stock market and can teach you lessons that will make you a savvier investor. Downturns and crashes are inevitable, and it is often difficult to stay disciplined and make decisions rooted in reason rather than emotion when they occur.

Before we dive into the past, it'll be helpful for you to understand some relevant terminology:

- **Bull:** A bull is someone who is optimistic or *bullish* about the future of the stock market. A bull market is a sustained period during which stocks have been gaining value. It typically indicates that the economy is healthy and growing and that investor sentiment is positive.
- **Bear:** A bear is someone who is pessimistic or *bearish* about the stock market and believes it will go down. A bear market occurs when the stock market declines 20 percent or more from its peak. The average bull market is longer than the average bear market, which is why you can grow your money over time through investing in the stock market.
- **Correction:** A market correction occurs when the stock market drops by 10 percent or more.
- **Index:** You may remember indexes from Chapter 11. As a refresher, a market index is a group of stocks used as a benchmark for market performance. The Dow Jones

Industrial Average includes thirty of the most influential and well-established companies in the United States, while the S&P 500 consists of the five hundred largest publicly traded companies in the United States.

- *Recession:* A period during which the economy is experiencing stagnant or declining economic growth, usually denoted by a decline in *gross domestic product* (the monetary value of all goods and services produced in a nation) that lasts at least two consecutive quarters.

FINANCIAL TALES

THE DUTCH TULIP CRAZE

Referred to as "Tulip Mania," the Dutch tulip bubble didn't have anything to do with stocks. However, it is a classic example of a major financial "bubble." A bubble occurs when the price of a commodity or asset becomes untethered from fundamentals (aka it costs significantly more than it is worth). Speculation leads to inflated prices. Oftentimes, a bubble follows a basic path. First, an asset becomes popular. Then, a boom occurs as people rush to buy it, influenced by their fear of missing out on what they perceive as a golden opportunity. Demand exceeds the supply, and the price of the asset surges. Once the price of the asset peaks, people decide to take profits by selling their investments. This has a domino effect, and the bubble bursts. Oftentimes, it is not apparent when the speculative price surge associated with a bubble is occurring; it is only after the bubble bursts that it seems obvious.

In seventeenth century Holland, the Dutch fell head over heels for tulips. The extremely high demand fueled a surge in the prices of tulip bulbs. People began exchanging their assets for bulb. In fact, many individuals bought the tulips on credit, planning to repay their loans after selling the tulips for a profit. The bubble burst in 1637, however. Once some investors began to sell the tulips to turn a profit, a slew of others followed suit. Tulip prices slid amid the selloff as panic-stricken investors tried to minimize their losses.

THE GREAT DEPRESSION

NARRATIVE

The Stock Market Crash of 1929 ended a decade of rapid economic and social growth called the Roaring Twenties which followed the American victory in World War I and effectively plunged the United States into the Great Depression. After the war, Americans were euphoric, believing that "the war to end all wars" had been won and that good times would permanently ensue. Stocks became markedly overvalued, and many Americans were leveraged. Soon, indications of a downturn began to surface. Diminishing international trade, decreasing steel production, and climbing unemployment rates signaled the end of the economic boom. The wealth gap was ballooning; it is estimated the top 1 percent of America's population held 19.6 percent of its wealth.

The stock market soon began to adjust to the economic reality. The precipitous market crash began on October 24, 1929 and ended on October 29, 1929, a day now infamously referred to as Black Tuesday. Over sixteen million shares of stock were traded on that single day. However, the largest decline in the stock market occurred over the following two years as the Great Depression fully materialized. In 1932, the Dow Jones Industrial Average bottomed out, having fallen 89 percent from its September 1929 peak.[41]

During this same time period, a series of droughts called the Dust Bowl swept the Southern regions of the United States. Farmers had no hopes of agricultural livelihood, as their land was ruined.

Unemployment rates rose and GDP declined. As financial panic set in, Americans dashed to banks with the intention of withdrawing their money. However, many overwhelmed banks lacked the cash to fulfill the massive number of withdrawals, leading to many shutting down (this problem preceded the creation of FDIC protection). Additionally, many small businesses felt a great deal of pain as they didn't have the resources to continue operating and were forced to declare bankruptcy.

REBOUND

America began the road to recovery shortly after Franklin Delano Roosevelt was inaugurated. Roosevelt began implementing policies that were part of the "New Deal." Unemployment levels dipped and federal spending significantly increased as the United States fought World War II in the early 1940s. It is commonly believed the Dow Jones did not return to its 1929 high until November 1954. However, some

---

41   Clay Halton, "Black Tuesday," *Investopedia*, updated January 9, 2021.

experts suggest that it actually took significantly less time for the market to rebound. The analysts that make this case maintain that someone who invested in an average stock at the market's 1929 high would have been able to recoup their losses by late 1936, less than four-and-a-half years after the mid-1932 market low.[42]

THE BEAR MARKET OF 1973–74

NARRATIVE

A confluence of factors engendered the second-longest bear market in history. As the post-World War II boom began to end, economic growth dwindled, and the inflation rate sat at well over 11 percent. This simultaneous decrease in economic growth and high inflation rate is dubbed "stag-flation." Wages began to stagnate. American confidence decreased amid the Watergate scandal and the United States' failed intervention in Vietnam. Furthermore, in 1973, the Organization of the Petroleum Exporting Countries (OPEC) imposed an oil embargo against the United States in response to the nation's support for Israel. This embargo revealed the US' overdependence on oil, and the prices of oil concomitantly surged.

The steep stock market decline began in early 1973. On January 11, 1973, the Dow peaked at 1,052 points. On December 6, 1974, the Dow bottomed out at a twelve-year low of 578.

---

42 Mark Hulbert, "25 Years to Bounce Back? Try 4 1/2," *New York Times,* April 25, 2009.

REBOUND

On April 27, 1981, the Dow closed at an eight-year high of 1,024 points. For reference, as of April 2021, the Dow was well over 34,000 points. Patience pays.

BLACK MONDAY—OCTOBER 19, 1987

NARRATIVE

Black Monday was a testament to the degree to which international markets had become closely linked. On October 19, 1987, the Asian markets crashed, and the ensuing panic spread to financial markets around the world. Shortly after the markets opened in the United States on Monday morning, the Dow crashed. Although the crash began in Asia, there were warning signs in the United States that a market decline was imminent. For one, stock prices had rapidly surged; within the first seven months of 1987, the Dow Jones Industrial Average had gained 44 percent. The introduction of digital trading systems led to swift selling; stocks were quickly traded in large volumes, which stoked volatility and added to the decline. Additionally, the government announced trade deficits were rising, which devalued the dollar.[43] Heightened tension in the Persian Gulf is cited as a factor as well. As previously mentioned, this chain reaction of market crashes was a testament to how intertwined the global financial markets had become. The media displayed bleak images of stock traders, which elicited a predictable response from the general public. The more investors watched the media coverage

---

43   Donald Bernhardt, Marshall Eckblad, and Federal Reserve Bank of Chicago, "The Stock Market Crash of 1987," Federal Reserve History, November 22, 2013.

of the market crash, the more they felt inclined to sell their holdings. A selling frenzy ensued. By the end of the day, the Dow dropped 22.6 percent. Up to this point, this decline was the largest single-day percentage drop in history.

REBOUND

Losses were quickly recouped. In fact, the market posted a record one-day gain the next day, and the Dow reached its previous highs within less than two years. After the 1987 market crash, "circuit breakers" were implemented, which temporarily pause trading when the S&P 500 declines a certain percentage from the previous day's close. These measures were created to curb panic selling.

THE DOT-COM BUBBLE—1995–2001

NARRATIVE

In the 1990s, investors flooded internet startups with money, hoping to identify companies that would prove to be on the cusp of the future. Startups aggressively marketed in an attempt to differentiate themselves from competitors and draw new investors. In fact, some companies spent up to 90 percent of their budget on advertising. In some cases, companies that had yet to finish developing a product went public and their stock prices increased threefold and fourfold in a single day. By 1999, 39 percent of all venture capital investments were routed toward internet companies.[44] Between 1995 and 2000, the tech-heavy Nasdaq more than quintupled. The bubble was rooted in speculation. Investors threw

---

44   Adam Hayes, "Dotcom Bubble," *Investopedia,* updated June 25, 2019.

caution to the wind despite glaring red flags. As in previous crashes, many investors were extremely leveraged (i.e., they invested with borrowed money). To say the least, tech companies were overvalued.

The Nasdaq index peaked on March 10, 2000. The bubble soon burst, and investors began panic selling. By the end of 2001, many dot com companies were bankrupt and became virtually nonexistent.

REBOUND

The Nasdaq regained its prior peak in April 2015. The tech bubble exhibited the importance of diversification. It demonstrated that if you have a diversified portfolio (including some cash) consisting of solid companies with good earnings and fair valuations, market crashes can be tremendous buying opportunities. One of Warren Buffet's famous mantras is: "Be fearful when others are greedy and greedy when others are fearful."

THE GREAT RECESSION—2007–2009

NARRATIVE

In September 2008, Lehman Brothers filed for bankruptcy, setting off a chain reaction. Lehman was one of the most eminent and prestigious investment banks in the United States and was the first of several large banks to collapse.

Let's rewind a bit to understand the roots of the financial crisis. It all began when banks started to approve mortgages for home buyers who were financially unqualified.

These mortgages are referred to as "subprime," as they were issued to borrowers who were financially unfit. The banks made the mortgages appear initially cheap to borrowers but would then make them shell out larger monthly payments after the first few years. Eventually, many subprime mortgage borrowers defaulted on loans they were unable to afford, which financially devastated banks, as several had loaned money that would not be repaid. In addition, these banks had taken the money in their coffers and invested it in leveraged, risky bets. The housing and financial markets both collapsed.

The government eventually stepped in and bailed out banks and financial institutions that were deemed "too big to fail," as it feared that the collapse of the banks would imperil the entire financial system.

The S&P 500 lost over half its value between 2007 and 2009, and the United States gross domestic product (GDP) declined by 4.3 percent from 2007 to 2009. Millions of Americans were jobless as the national unemployment rate spiked. Most millennials can attest to the fact that they entered a less-than-optimal job market.

REBOUND

In October 2008, President George Bush established the Troubled Asset Relief Program (TARP) with the goal of allocating around $700 billion to aiding struggling banks and to stabilizing the financial system. In February 2009, President Barack Obama signed the American Recovery and Reinvestment Act, an enormous stimulus package that dedicated $787 billion to financial relief for Americans.

The Federal Reserve cut interest rates in an effort to stimulate consumption. After the crisis, Congress passed the Dodd-Frank Wall Street Reform and Consumer Protection Act in an effort to regulate financial institutions more stringently and to ensure they weren't making extremely risky bets. Lending standards were also tightened.

The Great Recession is considered to have ended in mid-2009 when employment rates began to increase, and the market began to recover. The S&P 500 bottomed out at 676 points in March 2009 and, as of April 2021, sat at well over 4,100 points (aka more than sextupled).

THE MARCH 2020 CRASH

NARRATIVE

Between February 12 and March 23, the Dow lost 37 percent of its value. In fact, on March 16 alone, the Dow dropped 12.9 percent as national lockdowns were instituted to prevent the spread of the COVID-19 virus. Anxious investors worried about that the pandemic could give rise to a recession. The rapid drop in stock prices triggered multiple trading halts that day.

REBOUND

A massive boom followed the sharp market downturn. The S&P 500 was notching fresh records by August, and the Dow exceeded thirty thousand points for the first time ever on November 24. The three major indices all ended 2020 with gains: the Dow gained 7.2 percent, the S&P 500 finished the year up 16.3 percent, and the tech-heavy Nasdaq composite index soared by 43.6 percent.[45] The market was led by big tech companies and was driven higher by investors' expectations that vaccines would soon be available, which would allow people to return to a semblance of normal life. This rally demonstrated the idea that the stock market is a forward-looking mechanism, as investors weren't focused so much on current conditions as they were on future expectations. The Federal Reserve, the Treasury Department, and Congress acted swiftly to support the ailing economy. The government pumped money into the economy in several forms, including unemployment benefits and stimulus checks. During the crash, online trading surged as many investors working and learning from home spent their newfound free time buying and selling stocks; brokerages saw large surges in trading volumes.

BECOMING A LONG-TERM INVESTOR

The main lesson from these stories is that the market *will* go down while you are an investor. However, the market's historical average 7 percent real return *includes* these bear markets. You may receive a 27 percent return on your investments one year, -16 percent the next, and 4 percent the following year. If you can separate yourself from your emotions, avoid panicking, and take a long-term approach to your investing, you will thrive in the stock market. The common thread between all the market crashes profiled is that the market always rebounded and investors who persisted thrived. If you buy good stocks when they are "on sale"

---

45   Jim Zarroli, "Stocks 2020: A Stunning Crash, Then A Record Boom Created Centibillionaires," *NPR*, December 31, 2020.

because everybody else is selling, you can trounce the average market return. Staying disciplined and taking advantage of downturns is easier said than done. It can be difficult to make rational decisions when you are staring at a screen full of bright red arrows. Luckily, there are a few strategies that can help you prosper.

DOLLAR COST AVERAGING (DCA)

Dollar cost averaging entails investing a set amount of money into one or more stocks or funds at a regular time interval. For instance, you could choose to invest fifty dollars every month. This strategy results in buying fewer shares when the market is up and more when the market is down. DCA adds discipline to your investing and can help protect you against market volatility. Karen Finerman remarks, "I am very much in favor of dollar cost averaging. Do anything you can to take the emotions out of investing because your emotions are almost always going to lead you astray." You can set up recurring investments with your brokerage.

BUY AND HOLD INVESTING

If you are a buy-and-hold investor, you buy stocks (or other securities such as ETFs) and hold them for a long period of time regardless of market fluctuations. In Morgan Housel's *The Psychology of Money,* he notes that Warren Buffett, often regarded as the best investor of all time, accumulated at least 95 percent of his wealth after age sixty-five. Housel explains that if Buffett had earned his extraordinary returns for only thirty years, he would be worth 99.9 percent less. He writes of Buffett, "The real key to his success is he's been a phenomenal investor for three quarters of a century. His skill is investing, but his secret is time."

Putnam Investments found that an individual who invested $10,000 in the S&P 500 in 2005 would have seen their money grow to $41,400 in 2020. The catch is that if the individual invested the same lump sum but missed the ten best days in the market, their money would only grow to $18,829. If they missed the thirty best days, they would actually lose money and end up with $7,526.[46] Therefore, time in the market is critical. Remember that you do not have to pick individual stocks to grow your wealth in the market. Investing the majority of your money in an S&P 500 index fund is a sound strategy and involves virtually no effort. The key is to not touch your money during downturns. Oftentimes, the market's worst days are followed by its best. You know how the saying goes—good things come to those who wait.

BUY LOW, SELL HIGH

Recall that there are two ways to make money in the stock market: by receiving dividends from the companies in which you are invested and/or by selling your investments at prices higher than those at which you bought them. Take advantage of bear markets by purchasing shares of quality companies at low prices. In fact, if you can, consider investing a bit more than usual. Then, down the road, you may be able to sell your investments for a profit.

---

46 *Time, Not Timing, is the Best Way to Capitalize on Stock Market Gains* (Boston, Massachusetts: Putnam Investments).

STAY INFORMED

Keep up with the news. Financial markets move in response to what is going on in the world. Pay attention to current events and not just to those that directly relate to the financial world. For example, during the pandemic, the market surged at times when vaccine trials conveyed promise and when world banks injected large amounts of money into the economy. Read reputable news sources, such as the *Wall Street Journal*, to which you can purchase a student subscription for as little as four dollars per month. Your understanding of the economy and the stock market will increase the more you read.

ADHERE TO YOUR PLAN

There is a reason you create a plan before you begin investing. You can't invest in stocks without thinking about how you will react if their value drops. When the market crashes, it's important to remember your time horizon and your goals. Because this book is written for members of Gen Z, you are probably relatively young. Retirement may be decades away for you, so don't stress too much. Know you have a plan.

DON'T PANIC SELL

Selling locks in losses or gains. If you have a long-time horizon with a well-balanced, diversified portfolio of solid companies, it is generally recommended that you not sell when the market is down. Of course, it is a different situation if you are invested in an individual company that appears as if it is headed underwater.

Take it from Jennifer Barrett, chief education officer of Acorns: "In the summer of 2008, I volunteered for a severance package when I was working at Newsweek. I made a deal with myself that I would primarily invest that money in the stock market, begin freelancing, and not touch the money. I invested almost all the money in index funds that mirrored major stock market indices like the S&P 500, the Dow, and the Nasdaq. Two months later, the financial crisis started, and the market dropped significantly. As I watched my investments drop 50 percent, I had a moment of panic during which I thought, 'I can't believe I just put all of this money into the stock market.' But I was also writing about personal finance, and I knew throughout history the stock market has recovered from every downturn to grow significantly and to set new records. As hard as it was emotionally not to touch that money, I not only didn't touch the money, but I continued to put more money into my investment accounts. I didn't touch my investments, and the amount of money I invested in 2008 has more than tripled [as of 2020]. This experience was a huge lesson for me and reaffirmed my faith in the wisdom of investing in a diverse mix of stocks. It also reaffirmed my belief that it is a good idea to invest in low-cost index funds that mirror the major indexes because you are then essentially investing in the stock market as a whole. The experience serves as a reminder that the stock market can go up and down. It can fluctuate in the short run, but it has grown significantly over the long run. When you see the market dropping, you likely have an emotional reaction, so it's really important to not panic sell and to remember investing is about the long game. Learning from history is a good reminder that the stock market can go down and can be bumpy; it's not a straight line up. But when you zoom out and look at the historical growth of the stock market, it is an incredible and upward trajectory."

∗∗∗

The key takeaway from this chapter is that the vicissitudes of the stock market are natural. At times, investing in the market can feel like riding a rollercoaster with your eyes closed. The market can go up and down in violent swings, so it is important to respect its volatility. JJ Kinahan, chief market strategist at TD Ameritrade, comments, "I was twenty-three when the Crash of 1987 occurred. I was trading at the time. A [downturn] affects how you think about the market forever—not necessarily in a bad way, but in a more respectful way."

There will be moments when you will want to jump for joy and others when you will just want to climb into bed and eat a pint of ice cream. However, you must understand the stock market is cyclical, and, like practically everything in life, ups and downs are only temporary.

FUN FACTS

- The terms "bull" and "bear" are derived from the way the animals tend to attack; a bull thrusts its horns upward, while a bear swipes its paws downward.
- The Super Bowl indicator is a theory that the stock market's annual performance can be predicted by which team wins the Super Bowl. A win from a team in the American Football Conference (AFC) supposedly foretells a bear market in the coming year, while a win from a team in the National Football Conference (NFC) is thought to prognosticate a bull market in the coming year.

Z NOTES

- A bull market is a period during which the prices of stocks are generally rising, while a bear market is a period during which stocks are generally losing value.
- The market has historically always recovered after a financial downturn.
- Avoid panic selling. Take advantage of market declines by investing in strong companies with good fundamentals.
- Dollar cost averaging is a strategy that can add discipline to your investing. It involves investing a set dollar amount into stocks and/or funds at a regular time interval.

PART 4

MODERN MONEY

CHAPTER 16

Doing Well While Doing Good: ESG Investing

———

"Ultimately, purpose is the engine of long-term profitability."

—*LARRY FINK, CEO OF BLACKROCK (THE
WORLD'S LARGEST INVESTMENT FIRM)*

Recycling, donating, protesting, volunteering, investing—
which of these is unlike the others? When it comes to making
the world a better place, investing is probably not the first
thing that comes to mind. However, it has a bigger impact
than you might think. Luckily, there has never been a time
during which being socially conscious and having a desire
to build wealth fit so well together as they do today. In fact,
investing with the social good in mind is more accessible
and profitable than ever.

Environmental social governance (ESG) investing entails factoring in a company's values and practices as they pertain
to environmental impact, relationships, and leadership in

addition to its financials when making an investment decision. Once considered fairly niche, ESG investing has rapidly gained traction over the past decade.

A 2019 Morgan Stanley survey found that 85 percent of individual investors are interested in sustainable investing, an increase from 75 percent just two years earlier.[47] Additionally, in 2019, Bank of America predicted that another $20 trillion would flow into ESG funds over the next two decades, which the firm called a "tsunami of assets." For context, the entire S&P 500 was worth approximately $25.6 trillion at the time of the prediction.[48] Furthermore, Bank of America's 2020 "Ok Zoomer" report found sustainability to be important to Gen Z consumers, and also discovered that Gen Z focuses on environmental and social issues across all facets of life. In fact, the firm discovered that 80 percent of Gen Z factors ESG criteria into investing decisions.[49] Let's dive a little deeper into this socially conscious way of investing.

E—ENVIRONMENTAL

The environmental element of ESG investing consists of a variety of factors that represent how a company interacts with and impacts the Earth. Topics you may research as they pertain to a company include:

---

47 Morgan Stanley Institute for Sustainable Investing, *Sustainable Signals: Individual Investor Interest Driven by Impact, Conviction and Choice*, 4.

48 Pippa Stevens, "Your Complete Guide to Investing with a Conscience, a $30 Trillion Market Just Getting Started," *CNBC,* December 14, 2019.

49 Bank of America Corporation, *OK Zoomer: Gen Z Primer* (Charlotte, North Carolina: BofA Global Research Thematic Investing Report, 2020), 4.

- Recycling and disposal practices
- Carbon footprint
- Packaging material
- Environmentally friendly products and services
- Use of renewable energy
- Land conservation and usage
- Water conservation and usage

S—SOCIAL

The social element of ESG investing is grounded in a company's relationship and interactions with its stakeholders. Stakeholders are individuals or groups that impact or can be impacted by a company. They include, but are not limited to, employees, customers, and suppliers. Annual lists, such as *Fortune's* Best Companies to Work For, provide insights that can prove useful in evaluating the degree to which a company adheres to this aspect of ESG investing. Topics you may research as they pertain to a company include:

- Employee compensation and benefits
- Hiring practices
- Company culture
- Product quality and safety, history of recalls
- Consumer protection and privacy
- History of lawsuits

G—GOVERNANCE

The governance element of ESG investing relates to corporate management. Topics you may research as they pertain to a company include:

- Transparency in communication
- Management diversity
- Executive compensation

THE SUSTAINABLE INVESTING MOVEMENT

As challenges such as climate change and data privacy become increasingly central to how companies operate, they are facing rising complexity. Given these pressing challenges, investors are reevaluating traditional investing approaches. They want to support companies with values that align with their own, while simultaneously deriving financial benefit from their investments. For instance, an investor concerned about sweatshops may not want to support companies contributing to the issue. Rather, they might invest in a company with a history of fair labor practices.

Issues such as climate change and inclusion are of particular importance to Gen Z, and there is an immense demand from our generation for sustainable and ethical investment options.

BlackRock—the world's largest asset manager—has been a major force paving the way for the sustainable investing movement. In a letter to CEOs, chairman and BlackRock CEO Larry Fink wrote, "Young people have been at the forefront of calling on institutions . . . to address the new challenges associated with climate change. They are asking more of companies and of governments, in both transparency and in action." He continued, "The importance of serving stakeholders and embracing purpose is becoming increasingly central to the way companies understand their role in society . . . a company cannot achieve long-term profits without embracing purpose and considering the needs of a broad range of stakeholders. A pharmaceutical company that hikes prices ruthlessly, a mining company that shortchanges safety, a bank that fails to respect its clients—these companies may maximize returns in the short term. But, as we have seen again and again, these actions that damage society will catch up with a company and destroy shareholder value. By contrast, a strong sense of purpose and a commitment to stakeholders helps a company connect more deeply to its customers and adjust to the changing demands of society."[50]

Fink wrote the letter in 2020—the year the COVID-19 pandemic swept the world. The pandemic served as a catalyst for the mainstream adoption of ESG amid the increased focus on stakeholders during the crisis. Companies that align themselves with ESG factors are often those that are positioning themselves to thrive in the future. Companies concerned with strong ESG factors tend to be dynamic, innovative, and problem solvers. A commitment to ESG practices can foster a sense of shared purpose and responsibility within a company. It can also diminish risk in many ways. For example, a company with sound social policies may avoid employee turnover, which necessitates spending money training new employees.

Utilizing an ESG framework to make investment decisions can help investors pinpoint risk factors that are not easily identifiable with traditional evaluation frameworks. In 2015, German auto manufacturer Volkswagen faced fallout after

---

50 Larry Fink, "A Fundamental Reshaping of Finance," *Blackrock,* accessed July 7, 2020.

admitting defective devices were installed on eleven million of its vehicles to cheat on emissions tests. Prior to the scandal, Volkswagen's overall governance score was in the bottom twenty-eighth percentile of companies studied by MSCI ESG Research globally. Similarly, Equifax had a massive personal information breach, but major ESG data providers flagged security and privacy issues around a year prior to the breach and subsequently downgraded the company. These scandals highlight the benefits of ESG analysis.[51]

More and more companies have begun to adopt sustainable practices and increase diversity. In January 2020, investment bank Goldman Sachs announced it would not help companies IPO unless they had one or more "diverse" directors on their boards. According to Vanguard, eleven thousand companies report on how they incorporate ESG principles into their business operations, and 125 organizations generate research on the ESG investment landscape.[52]

One common concern associated with socially conscious investing is the perception that this strategy compromises investment returns. However, the reverse is true. Bank of America found that if one invested in companies with above average environmental and social principles, they would have avoided over 90 percent of the bankruptcies seen in the S&P 500 during the time period analyzed. Additionally, 68 percent of companies' total value was attributed to "intangible assets," like brand reputation, in 2018—an increase of 38 percent

---

51 "Volkswagen Scandal Underlines Need for ESG Analysis," MSCI, accessed August 30, 2020.
52 "ESG Investing: Discover Funds That Reflect What Matters Most to You," The Vanguard, Inc., accessed August 29, 2020.

from twenty years earlier.[53] In 2020, many sustainable equity funds beat the S&P 500's 16.3 percent return. For example, the Vanguard ESG US Stock ETF returned 25.71 percent, and the iShares MSCI USA ESG Select ETF returned 24.64 percent.[54]

CASE STUDIES

Please note the companies profiled in this section are not necessarily perfect but have taken numerous actions that reflect their commitment to positive social impact.

APPLE

"We believe business, at its best, serves the public good, empowers people around the world, and binds us together as never before."
—*APPLE CEO TIM COOK*

Here are a few of the ways Apple has and continues to become socially conscious:

- Working toward a goal to become carbon neutral across its entire business by 2030, meaning every Apple device sold will have a "net zero" climate impact.
- Established a $100 million Racial Equity and Justice Initiative, which aims to address education, economic

---

53 Bank of America Securities, *"10 Reasons to Care About Environmental, Social, and Governance (ESG) Investing"* (Charlotte, North Carolina: Bank of America Corporation, 2020).

54 Jon Hale, "Sustainable Equity Funds Outperform Traditional Peers in 2020," *Morningstar,* January 8, 2021.

equality, and criminal justice reform. Apple has developed an Impact Accelerator that invests in minority-owned businesses under the umbrella of this initiative.

- Has robots that recover key materials from iPhones.
- Focuses on low-carbon product design.
- Has commitments from over seventy suppliers (as of this writing) to use 100 percent renewable energy for Apple production. A press release describes, "Once completed, these commitments will avoid over 14.3 million metric tons of CO_2 annually—the equivalent of taking more than three million cars off the road each year."
- Supporting the development of the first direct carbon-free aluminum smelting process through investments and collaborations with aluminum suppliers.
- Invests in the global restoration and protection of forests and natural ecosystems.
- The company's stores, offices, and data centers are powered by 100 percent renewable electricity.[55]

MICROSOFT

"At its core, responsibility is about earning and sustaining the trust of the customers and partners we empower, and the communities in which we live and work. Without trust, none of our progress is possible."

—*MICROSOFT CEO SATYA NADELLA*

---

55   "Apple Commits to Be 100 Percent Carbon Neutral for Its Supply Chain and Products by 2030," Apple Inc. press release, July 21, 2020, on the Apple Inc. website.

Here are a few of the ways Microsoft has and continues to become socially conscious:

- Established a social investment model through which incremental revenue is reinvested into causes for social good, such as affordable housing.
- Makes some of its technology free for non-profit organizations.
- Transparent about data collection.
- Doesn't use email, chat, files, or other personal content to target ads.
- Partners with nonprofits to train teachers and students in computer science.
- Has been carbon neutral since 2012 and commits to being carbon negative by 2030.
- Builds tools and services that monitor and model impacts from climate and human behavior, which help people better understand the ecosystem around them.
- Retains membership in the Water Resilience Coalition, which is an initiative of the UN Global Compact CEO Water Mandate. Member companies have pledged to work collectively on water issues.
- Participates in product recycling programs.
- Handles and disposes of waste using environmentally responsible methods.
- Committed to responsibly sourcing raw materials.
- Engages and periodically communicates progress to shareholders regarding objectives.
- Belongs to more than one hundred fifty producer-responsibility organizations globally.[56]

---

56 "Corporate Social Responsibility," *Microsoft Corporation*, accessed October 6, 2020.

HOW TO FOLLOW AN ESG FRAMEWORK

- **Positive screening:** Seek companies that meet a positive standard, such as having a female executive.
- **Negative screening:** Rule out companies from your portfolio that engage in practices which make you uncomfortable. For example, you could choose to avoid companies that manufacture weapons or that sell tobacco products.

You can integrate ESG into your portfolio by picking individual stocks and bonds and/or by investing in ETFs and mutual funds. Some ETFs focus on particular causes, such as the SPDR SSGA Gender Diversity Index ETF (SHE) and the Invesco Solar ETF (TAN). Although investing in an ETF is convenient in that someone else is researching companies, picking individual stocks allows you to invest in companies that adhere to your personal criteria. If you choose to invest in an ETF, be sure to pay attention to the fund's holdings.

Many research firms have developed rating systems that score companies on ESG factors. One such firm is Morgan Stanley Capital International (MSCI). MSCI rates companies on a AAA to CCC scale. These ratings are reflective of how the company manages its industry-specific ESG risks and the company's ability to manage those risks relative to similar companies. AAA is the best score a company can receive, and CCC is the worst score a company can receive. *Morningstar*'s Sustainalytics is another research firm that ranks companies based on how well they adhere to ESG criteria. The ratings measure a company's unmanaged risk. They range from negligible to severe. There are two primary dimensions to Sustainalytics' ESG ratings: exposure and management. Exposure refers to a company's vulnerability to ESG risks, while management refers to the actions a company has taken to manage a specific ESG issue.

Many businesses also provide detailed information and reports on their websites that outline their ESG-related initiatives and successes.

Some robo-advisors, such as Betterment, offer pre-built socially responsible portfolios.

***

ESG provides a framework for our generation to mobilize our investment dollars in a way that earns us solid returns while also accelerating real social and environmental change. By investing through the lens of social impact, your portfolio can reflect your vision for the future.

FUN FACTS:
- California fines companies with all-male corporate boards $100,000.
- Sustainable investing began with religious groups such as Muslims, Quakers, and Methodists who set ethical parameters on their investment portfolios.[57]

---

57   Jess Liu, "ESG Investing Comes of Age," *Morningstar.*

Z NOTES:

- Environmental Social Governance (ESG) investing entails factoring in a company's values and practices as they pertain to environmental impact, stakeholder relationships, and leadership in addition to its financials when making an investment decision.
- You can adopt an ESG approach by screening individual companies and investing in their stocks and/or by investing in ETFs and mutual funds.

CHAPTER 17

Investing for
the Masses

———

*"A penny here, and a dollar there, placed at interest, goes on
accumulating, and in this way the desired result is attained. It
requires some training, perhaps, to accomplish this economy,
but once used to it, you will find there is more satisfaction in
rational saving than in irrational spending."*

—P. T. BARNUM

Investing is *not* just for the wealthy. In recent years, brokerage firms have revamped their business models in a way that
has gained traction among millennials and Gen Z. As a result,
the notion that investing is inaccessible and reserved for the
affluent has been disproved.

Sahil Bloom, an investor and financial education contributor,
reflects, "I think the idea of democratizing access to financial
markets and to the world of finance is a phenomenal one, and
it is essential to the continued progress of our country and

society in general. Personally, I think we should have as few barriers to entry as possible. Investing used to be reserved for the 'elite' classes and the wealthy. The idea that anyone can take control of and manage their own finances, and have access to robo-advisors, personally managed accounts, etc., is a powerful one. But it needs to be paired with education. Access is great, but you need education plus access to make it truly lasting. There's an entire new wave of interest from young people entering the financial markets, and they need to be educated around these topics so they can succeed and grow their wealth because it is a powerful thing for economic development more broadly. It's also powerful for equality in our culture and society."

Financial services company Robinhood, named after the famous figure who robbed the rich to give to the poor, pioneered commission free trading and democratized investing (made it available to anyone, regardless of income) for millions of people in the process. *Commissions* are fees charged by brokerages for buying and selling stocks and other securities. In October 2019, brokerage firm Charles Schwab announced it was eliminating commissions, which were previously $4.95, for buying and selling stocks online. Shortly after Schwab's announcement, other large brokerage firms, including Interactive Brokers, TD Ameritrade, Fidelity, and E*TRADE, followed suit and did away with commissions, which effectively made trading stocks free. Individuals can now invest small amounts of money more frequently without paying an exorbitant fee that is a large portion of the amount they are investing. After all, who wants to pay $4.95 when buying $20 of Apple stock? That being said, it is important to realize that frequently trading stocks does not necessarily translate to high long-term returns. The elimination of commission fees simply gives you the freedom to invest your money without worrying about paying a fee each time you place a trade.

In addition to slashing commissions, several brokerage firms have eliminated minimum account balances. In the past, many individuals were unable to invest in the stock market because they were required to have thousands of dollars to open and maintain an account. Jennifer Barrett, chief education officer of Acorns, comments, "When I first started my career, you needed to have $5,000 to open an investment account. It really was a barrier to investing and reinforced the idea that you had to have a certain amount of money before you could begin. A lot of fintech companies like Acorns have worked really hard to remove that barrier and make investing accessible for everyone for a lot less money."

Fintech companies have also paved the way for individuals to be able to invest small bits of money by purchasing *fractional shares*. Fractional shares are just what they sound like: fractions or pieces of whole shares of stocks and funds. A share is to a pie as a fractional share is to a slice of pie. Say you want to own stock in Apple and it is trading at $150, but you only have $30. Fractional shares enable you to purchase one fifth of a share of that company—you own a slice of the Apple pie.

Several brokerages offer the ability to purchase fractional shares, although the programs go by different names. For example, Charles Schwab calls its program Stock Slices, while Fidelity calls its program Stocks by the Slice.

If you own a fractional share of a company's stock, you get the same benefits (proportionally) if the stock rises and risk losing as much (proportionally) if the stock falls as you would if you owned a full share of the company's stock. If you purchase fractional shares of a stock that pays dividends, you receive dividends proportionate to the amount of stock you own. For example, if a company pays shareholders a two-dollar dividend for each share they own and you own half a share, you receive a one-dollar dividend.

Fractional shares offer many benefits to Gen Z investors. In the past, individual investors who could not afford a full share of stocks or funds had to wait until they could scrape together enough money. The price of a single share of stock can be quite expensive. As of this writing, a single share of Amazon cost well over $3,200. In the past, when share prices rose, some investors missed opportunities to buy at good prices because they didn't have enough money to purchase full shares. That is no longer an issue. Fractional shares remove the price impediment to investing and are a great way to buy companies that are on your wish list but that don't necessarily fit your budget. Remember—I've said it before, and I'll say it again—time is your BFF (best financial friend) when it comes to investing and waiting to invest can be expensive. With fractional shares, you don't have to delay investing, as they enable you to build a diversified portfolio with small sums of money. Let's say you have two hundred dollars to invest. Instead of purchasing a single share of stock in one industry, you could spend twenty dollars to invest in ten different companies. In a nutshell, you have the freedom to choose which companies you want to invest in, but you don't have to wait until you have enough money to purchase an entire share of them. Instead of potentially losing money by investing in speculative penny stocks and low-quality companies, you can invest in strong companies you believe in. In other words, you can choose companies based on solid fundamentals instead of just price.

You could also use the ability to buy fractional shares as a way to explore companies in which you might like to invest. Perhaps you could begin investing in individual stocks with a small amount of money as a complement to low-cost funds (see Chapter 11). Of course, it's important to note that, although fractional shares enable you to invest small sums, you still risk losing money. Investing requires discipline and research, no matter the amount being invested.

Beginning to invest with fractional shares can be an invaluable learning tool. Building wealth and becoming financially literate transcend memorizing facts and formulas. Beginning your investing journey with small sums of money can teach you the mechanics of the stock market and allow you to learn from your mistakes without taking on excessive risk.

INVESTING APPS

Our smartphones are like our personal assistants. From reading the news, to navigating a new city, to arranging transportation, most things can be done via an app.

In the past decade, a plethora of investing apps have emerged, and well-established brokerages have developed their own mobile investing platforms. For example, TD Ameritrade's platform allows you to view customized watch lists, get detailed stock quotes, and track the market through a few taps on your Apple Watch. However, the world of investing apps does not end there. Micro-investing platforms are tailored to novice investors who don't have a lot of discretionary money.

As implied by the name, micro-investing apps allow you to invest small amounts of money. They were designed to make investing accessible for everybody, no matter how much money one has. Barrett explains, "One of the things I found so innovative and inspiring in the way Acorns was approaching investing was the idea of investing spare change, because it removes the traditional barriers people feel around investing, like not having enough money or being afraid of the risk. Once people began investing their spare change, we saw they would then set up recurring investments on top of that, so it helps address one of the most common problems: getting in the game in the first place and just beginning to invest."

Hungry for some money? If you were in the mood for a delicious gourmet ice cream treat while walking around town, and there were several great shops from which to pick, how would you decide where to go? Perhaps you would consider each shop's offerings—sundaes, sauces, toppings, waffle cones, etc. The flavor selection would certainly be important. And, of course, the price would matter too. We'll explore investing apps like you are considering ice cream shops. Ice cream parlors periodically expand their menus, just as micro investing apps tend to expand their offerings. Before selecting a micro investing platform, research the company yourself; the features listed were current as of this writing and may have changed. The three apps profiled all have different business models and features, so they should give you a good sense of the different types of platforms available.

ACORNS

THE SCOOP

- **Round-Ups:** Imagine you had collected all your loose change over the years from your daily purchases—books, groceries, coffees, juices, and meals out. You'd likely have a good amount of money saved up. This is the concept Acorns Round-Ups is based upon. Any purchase made from a linked account, debit card, or credit card is rounded up to the next dollar. For example, if you buy a Chick-fil-A sandwich for $3.55, the app can round up your purchase to $4 and invest the $0.45. The money is moved from your funding account. Once your Round-Ups add up to at least $5 from your linked account, the money is automatically invested in your Acorns Invest account.
- **Found Money:** This is Acorns' version of cash back rewards. When you shop with one of its hundreds of Found Money partners—including Sephora, Apple, and Walgreens—you receive bonuses that are deposited into your Acorns Invest account. When you need to purchase an item from a partner, simply open your Acorns app, navigate to the "Found Money" section, and click on the icon of the company from which you wish to buy the item. You will then be redirected to the company's website and a fraction of the value of your purchase will be added to your Acorns account.
- **Recurring Investments:** Acorns enables you to arrange recurring deposits into your portfolio.

- **Additional offerings:** In addition to a standard taxable brokerage account, Acorns offers Acorns Later, Acorns Spend, and Acorns Early. Acorns Later allows you to save for retirement; the app offers Roth, SEP, and traditional IRAs. When you sign up for Acorns Later, the app recommends a plan for you based on your goals, employment, and income. Acorns Spend is a checking account and debit card integrated with Acorns. It offers free bank-to-bank transfers and does not charge overdraft or minimum balance fees. The checking account is FDIC-insured up to $250,000. Spend also offers fraud protection and an all-digital card lock. Acorns Early is a custodial brokerage account that can be set up on behalf of children.
- **Education:** Acorns has a news site, *Grow,* and blends education into its platform. A section of its website called Money Basics has numerous articles covering various financial topics.
- **Job portal:** In partnership with Zip Recruiter, Acorns has a hiring portal that enables you to browse and apply for a job within the app.

FLAVOR SELECTIONS

- When you create an Acorns profile, the app suggests one of its five prebuilt portfolios based on your answers to a few questions. The portfolios weigh different ETFs from well-known investment management companies, such as BlackRock and Vanguard, based on risk tolerance and time horizon. The five portfolio choices are: Conservative, Moderately Conservative, Moderate, Moderately Aggressive, and Aggressive. Acorns automatically rebalances your portfolio to maintain its target allocation.

- There is no minimum to open an account, but the platform requires five dollars to begin investing in one of its five portfolios.
- Plans:
  - Lite: One dollar per month—Acorns Invest account (free for college students)
  - Personal: Three dollars per month—Includes an Acorns Invest, Acorns Later, and Acorns Spend account
  - Family: Five dollars per month—Includes an Acorns Invest, Acorns Later, Acorns Spend, and Acorns Early account[58]

PUBLIC

THE SCOOP

- **Social Aspect:** Public "makes the stock market social." The platform allows you to follow other investors and view the companies in which they invest. You can also join or start group chats with your friends to talk about companies and trends and exchange ideas.
- **Auto-reinvest Dividends:** Public allows you to re-invest dividends into the company that paid them out.
- **Commission free trading:** There are no commission fees for buying or selling investments on Public.
- **Safety labels:** The platform provides safety labels to a subset of stocks and ETFs with the objective of helping investors making informed decisions.

---

58 Information from acorns.com.

- **Education:** A section of Public's website is dedicated to educational articles that range from "How to Invest in E-commerce Companies" to "How to Know if a Stock is Risky." The website also has a robust investing glossary. You may choose to tune into Public Talks, a virtual event series about money and investing.
- **Fractional shares:** Public's goal is to make it easy for everyday investors to build wealth by owning pieces of the brands they love. You may begin investing with as little as five dollars.
- **Market Snapshot:** This feature of the app gives you a real-time-view of the market's performance. It shows you the percentage change in indexes, including the S&P 500, Nasdaq, Dow Jones, and Russell 2000, and tells you which stocks are making the biggest moves during trading hours.
- **Long-Term Portfolio:** Drag-and-drop companies you believe in for the long-term into a dedicated space, called the Long-Term Portfolio.
- **Tools:** Public offers a Capital Gains Tax Calculator, Fractional Shares Calculator, and Ticker Time Machine, which shows you what the investments you didn't make in the past would be worth today.
- **Themes:** The app curates lists, which group companies by themes. This feature allows you to invest in what you know or in what interests you. Example of curated lists include: Future Ed, Gaming & Esports, Blockchain Technology, Payments, Genetic Engineering, Green Power, and Women in Charge.
- **Detailed Company Information:** For a given company, Public provides its price chart, a company description, articles related to the company in the news, brands the

companies owns (e.g., Apple owns Beats), Wall Street Analyst ratings (these ratings range from strong buy to strong sell), analyst price targets, upcoming events relevant to the company (such as earnings), and financial stats.

FLAVOR SELECTIONS
- You can trade over five thousand stocks on Public and invest in popular ETFs from Vanguard, BlackRock, and other investment management companies.

PAY UP
- There are no costs associated with Public's platform, although you may choose to include an optional tip when you make a trade to support the company's commitment to *not* participating in the practice of payment for order flow.[59] Payment for order flow is a controversial practice. Put simply, it is compensation that a broker/platform receives when it routes its customers' trade to a third party, which executes the orders. This means that platforms that engage in the practice of payment for order flow benefit the more you trade.

ROBINHOOD

THE SCOOP
- **Commission-free trading**: No commissions charged on stock, ETF, cryptocurrency, and options trades.
- **Fractional shares:** Buy fractional shares of stocks and ETFs with as little as one dollar.

---

59   "Features," Public.com.

- **Robinhood Gold:** This feature offers investors the ability to trade "on margin," meaning you can invest with money loaned to you by Robinhood. Please be aware margin trading is very risky, and I do not recommend it. This offering is included in this section to give you a comprehensive overview of Robinhood's offerings.

- **Cash Management:** Robinhood offers a cash management account that pays 0.30 percent interest on uninvested cash. Your cash is eligible for FDIC insurance. The account comes with a debit card and free withdrawals from over seventy-five thousand ATMs.

- **Recurring Investments:** You can set up recurring investments, meaning the company will purchase fractional shares for you on a schedule you choose.

- **Robinhood Learn:** Robinhood's website has a vast library of free in-depth articles covering a variety of subjects ranging from basic personal finance concepts to technical investing topics.

FLAVOR SELECTIONS

- As of this writing, Robinhood offers individual stocks, exchange-traded funds, options trading, and cryptocurrency (including Bitcoin and Ethereum). Please keep in mind that options trading is risky. You should never invest in anything you do not understand. Before engaging in options trading, research the risks and educate yourself. We will explore cryptocurrencies later in this book.

PAY UP

- Customers who opt to participate in Robinhood Gold pay a five-dollar fee per month.[60]

Robinhood engages in the practice of payment for order flow, meaning it has an incentive to encourage you to trade. The more you trade, the more money it makes. The gamification of Robinhood's platform that makes it extremely easy to trade without a second thought, coupled with its engagement in payment for order flow, has led some people to criticize it.

A FEW TIPS

Be mindful when you use a micro-investing platform that charges fees. A $3 fee may seem relatively paltry, but it can quickly take a big bite of, and even negate, your earnings. For example, imagine you invest $10 each month and earn a 7 percent annual return. Compounded monthly, you make around $4.50 in returns. You invest with an app that charges a $3 monthly fee. The $36 in fees you pay over the course of the year puts you in negative territory. The whole point of micro-investing apps is to make investing more accessible for everyone, regardless of how much money one has. You do not need to invest a ton of money to break even and benefit from micro-investing platforms, but you need to be cognizant of the costs associated with using one that levies fees if you are only investing a small sum per month.

Additionally, investing a few dollars here or there won't be enough to reach large goals like retirement. Although

---

60 Information from robinhood.com.

investing a few dollars here and there is a great way to begin investing, it's imperative to invest larger amounts of money when you can. The more you invest, the larger the nest egg you can grow. Set up recurring contributions and invest lump sums whenever possible. You may consider using a micro-investing app in conjunction with investing through a traditional brokerage.

I also want to point out that micro-investing apps allow you to trade with a few taps. Although the simple interfaces are part of the reason why anybody can easily participate in the stock market, they can also make it easy to make quick, emotional investment decisions if you are not careful. When you buy and sell stocks and funds, ensure that you have sound rationale. You should be able to clearly explain why you are purchasing or selling.

At the end of the day, micro-investing platforms and apps can make investing seem less intimidating and serve as a steppingstone to frequently investing larger lump sums. They are not for everyone, but they can allow you to get a portfolio started with a relatively small amount of money and foster good saving and investing habits. Certainly, they have disproven the notion that you can't invest if you don't have a seven-figure net worth. Perhaps most important of all, they serve to empower people.

***

Fitness tools, such as smartwatches and pedometers, drive healthy behaviors, foster healthy habits, and encourage you to take charge of your overall physical fitness. They fit seamlessly into your life and make staying healthy part of your lifestyle. The same should go for investing; it should simply be a part of a financially healthy life. Luckily, this has never been easier. The dynamic of the market is changing. Apps have emerged that gamify the process of investing, and legacy brokerages have expanded their services to fit the needs of young people. Young, digitally native investors can dip their toes into the waters of the market and begin building wealth early. As you have learned in this book, small amounts of money add up. If you have the psychological hurdle of "I don't have enough money," I hope this chapter has shown you only need a few dollars to begin investing. In fact, all you really need is some spare change.

FUN FACTS
- The average commission in the late 1980s was forty-five dollars for a single trade.[61]
- Many young people began investing during the COVID-19 pandemic. In the first four months of 2020, Robinhood increased its customer base by around three million users.

Z NOTES
- Many brokerages and investing platforms have eliminated commission fees, essentially making trading stocks and funds free. The elimination of commission

---

61   Rob Wile, "Back in The Day, Brokers Got Away With Murder in Trading Commissions," *Business Insider*, March 31, 2014.

fees affords you freedom in how you invest your money, but frequently trading stocks does not necessarily make you a better investor.

- A fractional share is a piece (or fraction) of a share of a company.
- Fractional shares lower the barrier of entry to investing, giving people who cannot afford to pay high prices the opportunity to invest. They enable young people to take advantage of their greatest asset—time—and provide an opportunity for experiential learning.
- Many brokerage firms have eliminated minimum account balances.
- Access to the stock market has greatly increased. Gen Z can begin building wealth early with small amounts of money.

CHAPTER 18

Cash Is No Longer King

—

Imagine a world in which money only exists digitally. No piggy banks, no tip jars, no cash registers. Although it may seem like a fantasy, a cashless society is gradually becoming reality. In fact, going cashless was already a trend before COVID-19, but the crisis greatly accelerated this process. Of course, that doesn't mean cash will completely vanish, but it does mean it will become less prevalent as society increasingly relies on credit cards, debit cards, apps like PayPal and Venmo, and mobile wallets. Perhaps Amazon Go stores offer a glimpse into what a cashless society could look like. Instead of relying on cashiers, the stores utilize computer vision technology to record what customers select. Shoppers simply walk in, select the items they would like to purchase, and leave the store. Their cards are automatically charged. The way in which people exchange money with companies and with each other has been redefined by the advent of innovative technologies.

Over 50 percent of Gen Z uses digital wallets monthly, and over 75 percent uses other digital payment apps or P2P apps (like Venmo).[62] In a *Morningstar* survey of Zoomers in the United States, each respondent said they use at least one financial app, whether for budgeting, investing, financial news, money transfer, or digital banking. Sixty-three percent said they find financial apps useful—more than any other generation.[63]

Products such as investing apps and robo-advisors have their own virtues, but the world of digital money doesn't end there. Alternative payment methods are rapidly taking over and contributing toward the decline of cash.

MOBILE WALLETS

A mobile wallet is just like a physical wallet, but it is digital. It allows you to pay for things through an app and stores digital equivalents of numerous items a traditional wallet holds, such as gift cards and transit cards. There are a multitude of mobile wallets available from which to choose. Let's take a look at two popular ones.

APPLE PAY

- Exclusively available on Apple devices
- Enables you to make contactless and secure purchases in stores, in apps, and online
- Affords the ability to send and receive money in Messages

---

62 Jaime Toplin, "Banking & Payments for Gen Z Report: The Winning Strategies for Attracting the Next Big Opportunity—Generation Z," *Business Insider,* May 1, 2019.

63 Stan Treger et al., "Dispatches from Generation Z," *Morningstar,* June 2, 2020.

- Service is compatible with the vast majority of credit and debit cards from nearly all US banks
- Enables you to keep your boarding passes, rewards cards, gym membership card, student ID, and more in the app
- Apple also offers a credit card issued by Goldman Sachs
  - When you purchase something using your Apple card, you receive a percentage of your purchase back in Daily Cash.
- Spending totals are automatically added up on the app, and you can choose to review them by week or month. Color-coded categories make it easy to identify trends in your spending.

To begin, simply open the "Wallet" app and add your credit cards and debit cards to the app by following the instructions provided. When you make a purchase, you authenticate using a PIN, face ID, or touch ID. Your card number is not stored on your device or on Apple servers, and when you pay, your card number is never disclosed to merchants.[64]

GOOGLE PAY
- Check out quickly in stores or in apps
- Send money to friends and family
- View the total balance from all your linked accounts
- Receive reminders about upcoming bill payments
- Get weekly summaries of your spending, track spending trends, and see your expenditures at different businesses
- Receive cashback rewards on daily purchases

---

64 "Apple Pay," Apple.

Google Pay is very similar to Apple Pay. Simply download the app, sign in to your Google account, and add a payment method. Each time you open the app or make a payment, you must use your fingerprint, PIN, or face to verify your identity. The service encrypts transactions.[65]

BENEFITS OF MOBILE WALLETS

1. **Convenience**

You don't have to worry about forgetting your wallet, as you most likely carry your phone with you everywhere you go. When completing a transaction, simply open an app and hold your phone (or smartwatch) up to a point-of-sale terminal.

2. **Security**

Major mobile wallets are widely considered to be safe. Unlike a physical wallet, a mobile wallet carries no risk of being lost or stolen. If your phone was stolen, the thief would need to crack the password on the phone itself and then any additional identity verification measures, such as PINs or touch ID, to access the app. Mobile wallets encrypt their users' payment information, meaning that your information isn't compromised or shared with third parties.

PEER-TO-PEER (P2P) PAYMENT APPS

Whether it's paying a friend back for brunch or splitting the Netflix bill with roommates, many people frequently find themselves needing to send money to friends and family.

---

65   "About Google Pay," Google Pay.

Peer-to-peer (P2P) payment apps make sending and receiving money frictionless.

HOW P2P PAYMENTS WORK

Imagine you plan to see the latest action movie with your friend Eleanor this weekend. Eleanor texts you to let you know she purchased tickets for the two of you so you could sit together. After thanking her, you open your favorite P2P app, type your PIN, search your contacts for Eleanor's name, enter the dollar amount you owe her, and press send. Boom—you've repaid Eleanor in a matter of seconds. The money is added to Eleanor's account balance. She can leave it there to pay someone else, or she can transfer it to her bank account.

There are numerous P2P apps to consider. As noted above, Apple Pay and Google Pay both enable users to send and receive money. Let's take a look at a few other common platforms.

PAYPAL

This service is often associated with e-commerce. However, it also offers peer-to-peer money transfers. You'll need a PayPal account to get started. Then, as long as the person you are sending money to also has an account, you can use their name, email address, or phone number to send and request cash. PayPal enables its users to buy, hold, and sell crypto, as well as pay for goods and services with crypto.

VENMO

A subsidiary of PayPal, Venmo is a money transfer app with a social media aspect to it. You can add a note each time you pay a friend, and friends can like and comment on purchases. This app is perfect for transferring money to your roomies for rent or for surprising your friend with five dollars for coffee. Venmo also offers a debit card that allows you to spend money from your Venmo account balance and earn cashback rewards at select retailers that are added to your account balance. You can check out with Venmo on some apps like Uber. Venmo enables you to buy and sell cryptocurrencies with as little as $1.

SQUARE'S CASH APP

Cash App affords you the capabilities of sending, spending, and investing your money. It allows you to receive, request, and send money to and from friends and family instantly. You can send money through your Cash App balance or through a linked credit card, debit card, or bank account. You can order a Cash Card (a customizable Visa debit card) from the Cash App, which allows you to spend the money on your Cash App balance and receive "cash boosts"—discounts automatically applied to a purchase when you shop with certain retailers. The Cash Card can be added to Apple Pay. You can deposit paychecks, tax returns, unemployment benefits, government stimulus payments, and more directly into your account. In terms of investing, Cash App offers commission-free investing in individual stocks and ETFs; you can begin investing with as little as one dollar. Additionally, the app allows you to buy and sell bitcoin. Note that, as of this writing, the platform just offers a standard, taxable brokerage account. It does not support IRAs or educational accounts.

***

Although a completely cashless society is not necessarily imminent, cashless payment systems are certainly becoming ubiquitous. Technology has driven a fundamental shift in how money is exchanged and transferred. As digital natives, Gen Z is open to alternative payment systems and our digital tendencies are catalyzing the cashless shift.

FUN FACTS:
- Cash may be dirtier than a toilet seat.
- Economists estimate only 8 percent of the world's currency exists as physical cash.

Z NOTES

- Cash is increasingly becoming less prevalent as people interact with money digitally through credit cards, debit cards, mobile wallets, and peer-to-peer payment apps.
- Mobile wallets are digital versions of traditional wallets. They can afford you convenience and security.
- Peer-to-peer payment apps make it quick and simple to send and receive money.

Cryptocurrency: Money 2.0

———

Over the course of thousands of years, the forms of money have evolved. To understand the digital forms of money prevalent in our modern world, it is important to first understand that money does not have real intrinsic value. Its value is dependent upon our perception of its worth. A dollar bill is simply a piece of cotton. Its importance is rooted in our belief it has value, as it is a medium of exchange.

Trading and bartering were precursors to the modern monetary system. They were means of exchanging goods and services, enabling all parties to get what they needed. For example, I could give you two sweet potatoes in exchange for an apple. The problem was that agreeing on the value of things proved difficult. Is a chair a fair trade for a horse? You could only determine the value of an item by knowing what people were willing to give you in exchange for it. Eventually, people began using mediums of exchange like shells, salt, and seeds that had standard values.

Around 600 BC, Lydia, a kingdom in present-day Turkey, was mining an alloy of gold and silver called electrum. One Lydian took pieces of electrum with consistent ratios of gold to silver, broke them into a standard size, and stamped an image of a lion onto each resulting chunk. Each piece had a standard unit value. The Lydians created coins. They soon began minting pure gold and pure silver coins. In 1000 AD, the Chinese invented the first forms of paper money.[66] Utilizing coins and paper money as mediums of exchange greatly simplified transactions.

At one point, the United States government backed up our currency with gold kept in vaults, which was called "the gold standard." As the economy grew, the government decided to stop backing its currency with gold. It claimed the money was backed by the "full faith and credit" of the United States.

Today, money has moved into a digital space. In the last chapter, we discussed cashless payment systems. As this digital transition has occurred, cryptocurrency has also become more mainstream.

Crypto
encrypted

Currency
system of
money

---

66 Jacob Goldstein, *Money: The True Story of a Made-Up Thing* (New York: Hachette Books, 2020), 9.

As the name implies, cryptocurrency is a digital and encrypted form of currency. Unlike traditional currency, it is not backed by a government. In recent years, cryptocurrencies have evolved from an object of fleeting interest into respected assets. In fact, the asset class has grown as a viable digital alternative to the money issued by governments. In some countries, governments can potentially seize their citizens' assets. Cryptocurrencies cannot be seized. Some experts posit they have the potential for economic empowerment, as they serve as a way for people around the world to participate in a global monetary system without being fully dependent on their government. Besides the popular Bitcoin, there are several types of cryptocurrency, such as Ethereum and Litecoin. Let's explore the differences between cryptocurrency and traditional (fiat) currency.

CONTROL

Governments issue and regulate fiat currencies. Fiat currencies are subject to currency manipulation by the governments that control them. The US dollar is a fiat currency. The Federal Reserve controls federal interest rates and the Treasury prints cash. Cryptocurrencies are not controlled by a government or by a central body.

SUPPLY

Many cryptocurrencies have predefined supplies. For example, the supply of bitcoin is capped at 21 million coins, which preserves its value. Governments control the supply of fiat currencies.

FORM

While cryptocurrencies only exist digitally, fiat currencies can exist both digitally and physically in the form of paper bills and coins.

PayPal has its own cryptocurrency service, which allows users to buy, sell, and hold cryptocurrencies. The company allows customers to use crypto to shop with millions of retailers. Venmo and Square also offer cryptocurrency services, and Fidelity established its own digital assets division, showing financial firms' increasing interest in cryptocurrency. Several businesses have issued their own currencies, which can be traded for the goods and/or services the company provides (this works similarly to tickets at the fair).

Both exciting and controversial, cryptocurrencies can be used to buy goods and services or can be held as investments.

Although holding cryptocurrencies affords you the potential for astronomical returns, it is important to understand the risks associated with investing in them, which include:

- **Volatility:** The price of cryptocurrencies can swing wildly. Cryptocurrencies tend to be significantly more volatile than stocks.
- **Bad actors:** Bad actors can attempt to hack into platforms like PayPal. They can even try to crack the code to access secure digital wallets, such as Trezor, in which digital currencies are stored.
- **No federal backing:** When storing traditional currency at the bank, you don't have to worry about it disappearing because banks are regulated, and your money is protected

by FDIC insurance. When it comes to cryptocurrency, it is up to you to securely store your funds.

BITCOIN

For a long time, gold has been considered the strongest form of money. It is durable and scarce, as it is difficult to mine. Gold isn't controlled by a single entity. A dollar in your wallet today can't buy you as much stuff as a dollar in your wallet twelve years ago could, as the purchasing power of the dollar has decreased. This phenomenon is called inflation. Excessive central bank money printing devalues fiat currencies. As there is a limited amount of gold in the world, it retains its value and is regarded as a hedge against inflation. In this way, gold primarily serves as a store of value (aka it doesn't depreciate and maintains its value).

However, there are inherent complications with gold. For one, it is difficult to securely store large amounts of it. After a certain point, storing it beneath your bed is no longer feasible or sensible. Additionally, it is difficult to divide gold into smaller units. Using it for daily transactions, like purchasing a book, is not realistic. For a long time, though, gold was the best hedge against inflation available. While not perfect, it was greatly advantageous in the sense that the government could not just print more of it with the tap of a button.[67]

Bitcoin functions sort of like "digital gold." Because its supply is capped at 21 million coins, some fans and experts predict that it will serve as a hedge against inflation. In 2020, as

---

67   Matthew Kratter, *A Beginner's Guide to Bitcoin*, chap. 1.

the US government took on massive amounts of debt, many people began investing in Bitcoin, fearing the value of the US dollar would significantly decrease. Bitcoin is designed to cut out third parties like banks. Going beyond borders, it is the first truly global currency.

"Bitcoin, and the ideas behind it, will be a disrupter to the traditional notions of currency. In the end, currency will be better for it."

—EDMUND MOY, 38TH DIRECTOR OF
THE UNITED STATES MINT

How to obtain
₿itcoin

Trade for goods and services   Purchase   Mine

- **Trade for goods and services:** You can receive Bitcoin by trading it for physical products and services. You can even earn it when you make purchases. Lolli is a browser extension that allows individuals to earn bitcoin when they shop online. The company has partnered with over one thousand brands and merchants, including Nike and Sephora.

- **Buy:** Similar to how you can exchange US dollars for the pound and other currencies, you can buy bitcoins with fiat currencies.
- **Mine:** In this context, mining is the process of verifying bitcoin transactions through solving complicated math problems. Once a miner solves a problem, a group of transactions is added to the blockchain, which we will discuss momentarily. Miners are rewarded with bitcoins. They expend immense amounts of computing and electrical power to solve the math puzzles. Mining for bitcoins is similar to mining in the real world; extracting a commodity like gold from the Earth takes time and effort.

To understand its evolution, let's look at a brief history of bitcoin:

2008—An author with the pseudonym Satoshi Nakamoto publishes a whitepaper entitled "Bitcoin: A Peer-to-Peer Electronic Cash System."

2009—The first bitcoin is created, which is dubbed "The Genesis Block." This is analogous to when the first US dollar was printed.

2010—The first bitcoin transaction takes place in the United States when a man in Florida purchases pizzas with bitcoins.

2017—The price of bitcoin climbs from below $1,000 to around $20,000.

2018—Bitcoin drops over 70 percent.

2021 (spring)—Amid a price surge, Bitcoin hits $1 trillion in market value and climbs to over $63,000.

2021- Coinbase IPOs.

Many major companies, such as Tesla, have invested in Bitcoin as an asset, lending it credibility. Additionally, as of this writing, the Bank of New York Mellon—the oldest bank in the United States—plans to hold, transfer, and issue bitcoins and other digital currencies on behalf of its asset-management clients. Morgan Stanley was the first major bank to allow its clients access to Bitcoin funds.

Twitter and Square CEO Jack Dorsey has said he expects Bitcoin to become the world's single currency in the future. However, for Bitcoin to become the currency of the future, its volatility will need to decrease so retailers can set consistent, fair prices for goods. Many experts postulate that as more and more people invest in Bitcoin, its price volatility will diminish.

I talked with Karen Finerman, cofounder and CEO of Metropolitan Capital, *New York Times* bestselling author, and panelist on CNBC's *Fast Money*, the day after Bitcoin broke $40,000 for the first time. She reflected, "In terms of dollars back per dollar invested, as of yesterday, it's the best investment I've ever made by quite a large margin. In terms of how big of an investment I made in bitcoin, it was not very large at all because I thought there was a very real chance my investment would be worthless." She states, "I think we could not be in a better environment to test the thesis of the risk of fiat currencies becoming worthless. More bitcoins will never be printed . . . we already know exactly how many bitcoins there will be. The thesis of what the Fed is doing now—just printing, printing money basically—is starting to play out. Simultaneously, you have an explosion in digital payments. Lastly, bitcoin is no longer considered a nutjob investment. As more institutional and well-known investors say they are taking a position in bitcoin, it gains the *Housekeeping* seal of approval for other investors to do that and have it in their portfolio. It's a really important evolution."

BLOCKCHAIN

Blockchain is a technology that functions as a data recording system. A blockchain is quite literally a chain of blocks. Each block represents a group of data or transactions. New blocks are added to the end of the "chain." Think of a blockchain like a large, shared Google spreadsheet, except information cannot be altered once it is entered. Entries made in a blockchain cannot be removed or edited. Let's look at Bitcoin as an example of how a blockchain works. When new transactions involving bitcoins occur, computers on the network solve math problems to verify these transactions. Valid transactions are added to the end of the blockchain. A block can be thought of as a box of donations for charity. Once you have enough items and clothes to fill the box, you send it in. Once there are enough transactions to form a block, the block is added to the end of the blockchain.

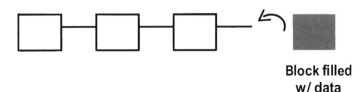

**Block filled
w/ data**

Blockchain is transparent in nature. Information in the blockchain is decentralized, as it is spread out over a large network rather than being stored in a single, central database. Each time a new entry is made in a blockchain, it is reflected on all the computers involved with running the network. "I think the whole idea of decentralization is a really important innovation, and the way it can be applied more broadly to the entire business and technological ecosystem is hugely valuable," says Sahil Bloom, an investor and financial education contributor. "When you think about a financial ecosystem that relies on all these gatekeepers and middlemen processing transactions, that's a lot of single-point-of-failure infrastructure. And it's worse than having a decentralized system that does not have a single point of failure."

POTENTIAL TO DISRUPT OTHER INDUSTRIES

Although blockchain is most commonly associated with the world of cryptocurrency, it has numerous other pragmatic applications and has the potential to disrupt and improve established systems across various industries. For example, blockchain technology could be used to create a digital, anonymous, secure voting system. Smart contracts are digital versions of physical contracts stored on blockchains. They can automatically perform specific actions, such as transferring funds, when predetermined stipulations are met.

Blockchain is also being leveraged for societal good. Facilities in the United Kingdom used blockchain technology during the COVID-19 pandemic to maintain a tamper-proof digital record of temperature-sensitive vaccines and note any irregularities in their storage.[68] Additionally, IBM partnered with a group of global food giants, including Nestle and Walmart, in an effort to harness blockchain to reduce food contamination. Essentially, IBM's blockchain network enables global food businesses to track the source of contaminated produce and enables food suppliers to source information about the origin, condition, and movement of food. As a result, food suppliers are able to trace contaminated produce in seconds.[69]

INVESTING IN CRYPTOCURRENCIES

Cryptocurrencies are high risk, high reward. They can compose a portion of a well-diversified portfolio if you can stomach their volatility. Before you invest in them, you simply need to understand what you are signing up for. JJ Kinahan, chief market strategist at TD Ameritrade, comments, "Do you understand the risk? We've seen $3,000–$4,000 moves in bitcoin. You have to ask yourself if you are comfortable with that. If you're going to invest in bitcoin, you have to be honest with yourself in terms of whether you are ready for the types of moves it has on a regular basis."

---

68 Ryan Browne, "IBM Partners With Nestle, Unilever and Other Food Giants to Trace Food Contamination With Blockchain," *CNBC*, August 22, 2017.

69 Ryan Browne, "UK Hospitals Are Using Blockchain to Track the Temperature of Coronavirus Vaccines," *CNBC*, January 19, 2021.

There are several ways to get exposure within your portfolio to cryptocurrencies and even blockchain.

You can invest in cryptocurrencies directly through a digital currency exchange, such as Coinbase. Digital currency exchanges are online platforms that allow you to buy and sell crypto. Remember that you can also purchase cryptocurrency through PayPal and Venmo and bitcoin through Square's Cash App. Just as you store bills and coins in a physical wallet, you should keep cryptocurrencies in a digital wallet. You are responsible for a private key (similar to a password) that gives you access to your wallet. You must keep your private key and recovery seed (password) in a safe place. If you lose them, you lose your assets. Individuals can use your address key, which is similar to an email address, to send you digital currencies. Keep in mind that, just as you can purchase fractional shares of companies, you can purchase a fraction of a "coin." If you wish to buy five dollars of bitcoin, you can do so.

Another way to get exposure to cryptocurrencies is to invest in a publicly traded company that is either invested in or facilitating the acceptance of cryptocurrencies. For example, as of this writing, Tesla holds $1.5 billion of bitcoin. Visa has partnered with Coinbase to issue a debit card called the Coinbase Card that enables investors to spend assets in their Coinbase portfolio. You can even invest in companies that leverage blockchain or that are creating products that support the cryptocurrency ecosystem. IBM has a division devoted to blockchain, and Nvidia creates chips that power bitcoin mining. You could also invest in a fund with exposure to crypto.

As a general rule, avoid investing in anything you don't understand. Jennifer Barrett, chief education officer of Acorns, advises, "Only invest the money you can afford to lose in cryptocurrencies. I have a very small percentage of my portfolio in cryptocurrencies because I find them fascinating. I think they are a little more fun . . . you have the opportunity to earn a lot of money, but they can also drop 10, 20, 30 percent in a very, very short period, which can be unnerving for investors."

Ultimately, there are various ways to get exposure to cryptocurrencies within your portfolio, but you do not have to invest in them to successfully build wealth.

***

As the cryptocurrency ecosystem burgeons, it is becoming increasingly clear that cryptocurrencies will play a role in the future of payments and in the global economy. Additionally, it is apparent blockchain will disrupt the way data is stored. It has the potential to improve established systems, as well as spur innovation for the social good. Ultimately, the advent and acceptance of digital currencies marks a monumental shift in the way we interact with money.

FUN FACTS

- Gen Zer Erik Finman became a millionaire as a teenager by investing in Bitcoin early on.
- Burger King launched its own digital coin in Russia called the "WhopperCoin." WhopperCoin tokens would be used to reward customers with each purchase of a Whopper sandwich.[70]

Z NOTES

- Unlike fiat currency, cryptocurrency is decentralized, meaning it is not issued by a single government or entity.
- Cryptocurrencies can be used to buy goods and services or can be held as investments.
- You can obtain bitcoins by purchasing, receiving, or mining them.
- Blockchain is a digital, transparent, decentralized record-keeping system. Once an entry is made in a blockchain, it cannot be altered.
- Blockchain has far-ranging applications across different industries.

---

70 Ryan Browne, "Burger King Has Launched Its Own Cryptocurrency in Russia Called 'WhopperCoin,'" *CNBC*, August 28, 2017.

Final Words

———

When I think of Gen Z, I think of transformation. Gen Z is driving change across all spectrums, reshaping the way things have traditionally been done and disrupting established paradigms. Through creating innovative solutions to pressing issues, we are generating real social impact. As the first generation of digital natives, Gen Z is revolutionizing the way people manage their finances through technology.

The United States has always prided itself on its ability to foster upward mobility and opportunity. America was founded on the ideals of capitalism, which is based upon the principle that all Americans can build wealth and better themselves through participating in the free market and benefitting from the growth and development of society. The underlying idea behind a company issuing shares of itself to the public was that anybody could build wealth through investing in the brands and businesses in which they believe. However, since the United States stock market was established in the late eighteenth century, this has not always been the case. For a long time, institutional investors have had disproportionate influence in the market compared to individual investors.

Only a small percentage of Americans have had the opportunity to build their wealth through investing. This power imbalance has begun to shift now that Zoomers are beginning to invest and make their voices heard in the traditional financial system. Individual investors are now beginning to increasingly influence not only individual stocks but also the overall market. As more Zoomers get involved in the market, this influence will only become more apparent as we strive to permanently displace traditional paradigms and level the unequal playing field. Our generation wants to both democratize investing such that all classes have the opportunity to benefit and smash the current cycle of the richest just getting disproportionately richer. Gen Z has enormous collective power—economically and otherwise—and is already living up to the prediction it will be the most disruptive generation ever.

We can apply the concept of change to our relationship with money. Gen Z can rewrite the traditional financial narrative and has the potential to be the most financially successful generation ever. We are not only navigating but also creating a new financial landscape. Between automation, fractional shares, money management apps, robo-advisors, and a wealth of information, financial success is more attainable than ever. Of course, Gen Z also has the most powerful force in the world on our side: time.

As you continue your financial journey after reading this book, I encourage you to view money as a tool and as a source of opportunity and freedom. Successfully managing your money means you control your finances rather than being controlled by them. Remember that little actions compound.

Saving and investing small amounts of money and creating good habits now will pay dividends down the road. Keep in mind the wisdom of Neale Godfrey: *your net worth is not your self-worth*. Your worth is not determined by a number or by opulent possessions but by the change you create and the impact you have on society. More than anything, I hope this book has empowered you to invest in your future.

Best of luck,
Ella

Resources Guide

Gen Z truly has a gold mine of information available with the tap of a button. However, with so much financial information available, it is important to be discriminating in choosing sources from which to learn. The below resources include those I have mentioned elsewhere in the book, so you don't have to flip through chapters in search of a specific tool.

EDUCATIONAL WEBSITES

- Investopedia.com: This site is like an in-depth financial dictionary. The content is fairly technical, but it is accessible for the most part. I recommend subscribing to Investopedia's "Term of the Day," which allows you to learn a new financial term every day.
- Nerdwallet.com: NerdWallet educates consumers about the various financial products and services available on the market through thorough reviews and comparison tools. It also contains digestible articles about various financial topics ranging from creating a budget to boosting your credit score. The website features several

calculators; two of my favorites are the Stock Market Crash Calculator and the Compound Interest Calculator.

- FINRA.org/investor: This site provides general overviews of basic investing and personal finance concepts, as well as tools and calculators.
- Investor.gov: This site run by the United States Securities and Exchange Commission features a lot of useful information for beginning investors and an excellent compound interest calculator, in addition to several other tools.
- Morningstar.com: *Morningstar* features educational articles and investing news. It also provides research on various investments and scores ETFs and mutual funds on a scale of one to five.
- Fool.com: The Motley Fool's website contains tons of informative investing articles and also provides product reviews and recommendations.
- Www.ngpf.org: Next Gen Personal Finance's (NGPF's) website is packed with resources for further learning.

DIGITAL EDUCATIONAL OFFERINGS FROM APPS, BANKS, AND BROKERAGES

Many brokerage firms and apps offer valuable free financial education resources. You can access all the resources below without being a customer.

- Acorns: Grow is an extension of Acorns' website. It features entrepreneurship tips and business news. Additionally, Acorns has a section of its website called Money Basics that contains a vast library of articles covering various personal finance and investing topics. I personally love Acorns' compound interest calculator.

- Bank of America: Bank of America's Better Money Habits®️ is a free resource that offers detailed, digestible information on topics such as home ownership and college.
- Fidelity: Fidelity.com/spire features articles ranging from "Refinancing Your Student Loan, Step by Step" to "How to Keep Money Resolutions." Fidelity also allows you to create a virtual mock portfolio. It created an app for young people called Spire, which allows you to invest, manage your finances, and view your Fidelity and non-Fidelity accounts in one place.
- Robinhood: Learn.robinhood.com has hundreds of in-depth articles covering a range of financial, economics, and technical investing topics.
- TD Ameritrade: The "Education" section of TD Ameritrade's website is robust. It features a range of educational articles. Each morning, a Daily Market Update is also published so you can keep track of the happenings on Wall Street.
- Wells Fargo: The "Financial Education" segment of Wells Fargo's website features basic information on the following topics: Basic finances, credit management, education finances, homeownership, investing, insurance and protection, and retirement.

Business Media
- Bloomberg
- CNBC
- *Financial Times*
- Kiplinger
- MarketWatch
- *The New York Times*
- Reuters

- TheStreet
- *The Wall Street Journal*
- Yahoo Finance

BOOKS

- *The Intelligent Investor*, Benjamin Graham: Warren Buffett's teacher, Graham is often recognized as the father of value investing. Graham's book about value investing was published in 1949 but has since been updated.
- *The Little Book of Common Sense Investing*, John C. Bogle: The founder of Vanguard, Bogle is credited with creating the first index fund. His book describes why buying and holding a low-cost index fund is the most simple and effective way to build long-term wealth.
- *One Up on Wall Street*, Peter Lynch: Lynch rose to fame in the 1980s as the fund manager of Fidelity Magellan. In this timeless read, he explains the advantages everyday investors have over professionals and how they can use these advantages to achieve financial success.
- *The Psychology of Money*, Morgan Housel: This book is interesting and highly entertaining. Housel argues that financial success isn't about what you know; it's about how you behave. He explains that people typically view money as math-based, but individuals do not make completely objective financial decisions on a spreadsheet. Rather, they make them at the breakfast table or in a meeting room, where their unique personal experiences and ego converge. In this book, Housel shares numerous short stories that explore the odd ways people think about and interact with money.

- *A Random Walk Down Wall Street,* Burton G. Malkiel: This classic book is packed with information. In addition to classic financial topics, it features interesting subjects like financial bubbles and behavioral finance. Additionally, the new version features topics relevant today, such as cryptocurrencies and tax-loss harvesting.
- *Too Big to Fail,* Andrew Ross Sorkin: This book is a deep dive into the Great Recession. The book is a product of over five hundred hours of interviews Sorkin conducted with individuals who participated directly in the events surrounding the financial crisis.

COLLEGE
- Federal Student Aid (studentaid.gov)
- www.collegeboard.org
- www.finaid.org

TAXES
- IRS.gov: You should be able to find out any and all information you need to know about taxes here, as well as guidelines for retirement accounts.

TOOLS

BUDGETING
- Mint: Mint is a money management app that allows you to budget, keep tabs on subscriptions, track your spending, and more.

- Trim: Trim analyzes your spending patterns and cancels old subscriptions. Additionally, it can negotiate your cable, internet, phone, and medical bills for you.
- Truebill: TrueBill monitors and cancels unwanted subscriptions, categorizes your expenses, and negotiates your bills.

CREDIT

- Credit Karma (Creditkarma.com): You can check your credit score for free.
- Annual Credit Report.com: You can view your credit report from Equifax, Experian, and TransUnion.

SHOPPING

- **RetailMeNot:** Use RetailMeNot's website or mobile app to find coupons, promo codes, and cashback offers. The platform also has a browser extension called Deal Finder™.
- **Honey:** Honey is a browser extension that finds coupons for you when you shop on 30,000+ sites.
- **Lolli:** Lolli is a browser extension that allows you to earn bitcoin rewards when you shop at 1000+ retailers, including Microsoft, Nike, Lululemon, Kroger, and Sephora.

Glossary

401(k)—An employer-sponsored, tax-advantaged retirement account.

529 savings plan—A tax-advantaged education investment vehicle that allows an account owner to save for a beneficiary's qualified higher education expenses and tuition for elementary or secondary school.

Annual Percentage Rate (APR)—When it comes to credit cards, the APR is the annual interest rate charged on one's outstanding balances.

Asset—Anything that has monetary value. Typical personal assets include stocks, bonds, art, cars, jewelry, and real estate.

Asset allocation—The process of deciding how much of an asset class and/or asset one would like to hold.

Bear—A person with a generally pessimistic outlook on the market, a market sector, or a specific stock.

Bear market—A period during which stocks are declining in value overall.

Beneficiary—Someone who receives money or other benefits from a benefactor. In the context of a life insurance policy, a beneficiary is an individual who receives a payout after the policyholder passes away.

Blue chip stock—A large, well-established, industry-leading company.

Bond—A loan that an investor makes to a party in need of money in exchange for interest payments.

Brokerage—A firm that acts as a "middleman" and buys and sells securities on an investor's behalf.

Bull—A person with a generally positive or optimistic outlook on the market, a market sector, or a specific stock.

Bull market—A period during which stocks are rising in value overall.

Capital gains—The profits that result from selling investments that have appreciated in value.

Cash advance—A short-term cash loan from one's credit card company.

Certificate of Deposit (CD)—A savings vehicle at a bank requiring a depositor to keep their money invested for a fixed period of time.

Collateral—A borrower's asset, which a lender may seize if the borrower fails to make loan payments as agreed. Collateral minimizes risk for lenders, as they can seize and sell the collateral to diminish its losses, should the borrower fail to uphold their end of the agreement.

Commission—A fee charged by a broker for executing a transaction.

Commodities—Fungible goods, such as grains, minerals, and gold.

Compound interest—Interest paid on principal and on accumulated interest.

Coverage limit—The maximum amount of coverage an insurance company provides in a given policy. Some insurance policies have multiple coverage limits that apply to the different types of coverage provided in the policy.

Copay—Separate from the deductible, a copay is a fixed amount of money an insurance company requires one pay out of pocket for each visit they make to the doctor. This fee is usually a relatively low, flat amount.

Credit history—A record of one's ability to repay debts.

Credit report—A statement that contains information about one's credit activity. This information is gathered by credit bureaus. The information in a credit report informs one's credit scores.

Credit score—A three-digit number that demonstrates one's creditworthiness (the likelihood of one repaying their debts).

Credit utilization ratio—The percentage of one's available credit they are using. In a nutshell, this is one's total outstanding credit card balances divided by all of their credit cards' credit limits.

Cryptocurrency—A digital asset that uses cryptography.

Custodial account—An investment account that belongs to a minor but is run by a designated adult until the minor reaches a certain age, at which point they may gain control over the assets in the account.

Deductible—The sum of money that must be paid out of pocket before insurance coverage kicks in.

Deduction—A deduction lowers a person's taxable income, allowing them to pay less in taxes.

- **Standard deduction**—A flat dollar reduction available to all taxpayers, regardless of individual circumstances.
- **Itemized deduction**—Allows someone to claim deductions that are specific to their personal circumstances.

Dependent—A person who relies on another as a primary source of income.

Direct tax—A tax collected directly by the government.

Discretionary income—The amount of money a person has left after their essential expenses are paid.

Diversification—The strategy of holding a mix of different types of investments to reduce the risk of a single holding imperiling one's portfolio.

Dividends—Payments made to shareholders from company earnings.

Dividend Reinvestment Plan (DRIP)—A program that enables investors to reinvest cash dividends they receive from a company to purchase additional shares or fractional shares of that company.

Dollar Cost Averaging (DCA)—DCA requires an investor to invest a set dollar amount each month, meaning they buy more shares when prices are low and less when they are high. This strategy can add discipline to one's investing.

Down payment—The lump sum paid up-front when one takes out a mortgage.

Earnings—A company's profits.

Effective tax rate—The average rate one pays on their taxable income.

Emergency fund—A stash of money set aside for unexpected expenses. An emergency fund is typically comprised of three to six months of basic living expenses.

Exchange Traded Fund (ETF)—A diversified group of securities. These funds are traded like stocks.

Expense ratio—The cost of owning shares of mutual funds and ETFs. This fee is generally expressed as a percentage of the investor's assets. For example, if an investor invests in a mutual fund with an expense ratio of 1 percent, they will pay $1 for every $100 invested.

Federal income tax—Federal income tax is a progressive tax, meaning people who earn higher taxable incomes pay higher federal income taxes. Based on the amount of taxable income a person generates in a year, they are placed in a tax bracket.

Federal Reserve—The central bank of the United States.

Fractional share—A part of one share of stock.

Grace period—The gap between the end of a credit card's billing cycle and when one's payment is due.

Gross Domestic Product (GDP)- The monetary value of all goods and services produced in a nation.

Index—A group of securities whose collective performance is used as a standard to measure the performance of the stock market. The S&P 500 index tracks the five hundred largest publicly traded companies in the United States.

Index fund—A passively managed mutual fund or exchange traded fund whose holdings match/track those of a particular market index.

Indirect tax—A tax collected by an intermediary. For example, sales tax is an indirect tax. This tax is collected by a store but is paid by customers.

Inflation—The increase in the price of goods and services over time and the resulting decrease in purchasing power.

Initial Public Offering (IPO)—Refers to when a company first sells shares to the public.

Insurance—A contract between two parties in which one party agrees to protect the other from financial loss.

Interest—The cost of borrowing someone's money.

Liquidity—How quickly or easily securities can be converted into cash.

Luxury tax—A tax charged on items considered nonessential and/or only affordable for very affluent consumers.

Market capitalization—A company's total stock market value, calculated by multiplying the current price of a single share by the total number of shares outstanding.

Micro investing—Investing in small increments by purchasing fractions of shares.

Mortgage—A loan taken out to purchase a home.

Mutual fund—A mutual fund pools money from several different investors and invests the money in numerous securities.

Net worth—The total value of one's assets minus the total amount of their debt.

Out-of-pocket maximum—A cap on the out-of-pocket money a policyholder will ever have to pay in a single year.

Overdraft—Occurs when an accountholder does not have enough money in their account to cover a transaction. An overdraft often triggers a penalty from the financial institution.

P/E ratio—The share price of a company's stock divided by its earnings per share (EPS) over the past year.

PEG ratio—The P/E ratio of a company's stock divided by its expected earnings growth rate. The PEG ratio can help an investor understand whether or not they are paying a reasonable price for a company in the context of its expected growth rate.

Penny stock—A term generally applied to stocks trading for less than $5 per share. Penny stocks are generally considered speculative and risky investments.

Portfolio—A mixture of investments.

Premium—The amount one pays to own an insurance policy.

Principal—The dollar amount of money deposited into an account or borrowed, not including interest.

P/S ratio—The market capitalization of a company divided by its revenue over the past twelve months.

Recession—A prolonged period of declining economic activity.

Revenue—The total amount of money a company generates through the sale of goods and services.

Risk tolerance—The extent to which an investor is comfortable with the prospect of losing money on an investment and to which they are able to deal with volatility.

Robo-advisor—An online service that utilizes an advanced algorithm to create and manage investment portfolios in an automated manner. Robo-advisors are generally more cost-effective for young investors than human financial planners.

Roth IRA—A tax-advantaged retirement account. Post-tax funds may be contributed to a Roth IRA, and money can be withdrawn tax-free in retirement as long as certain conditions are met.

Sector—A specific segment of the economy that encompasses companies with shared characteristics.

Securities and Exchange Commission—The federal regulatory body tasked with protecting investors and maintaining fair, efficient, and free markets.

Share price—The price at which a share of stock is currently trading.

Sin tax—A tax on items that are considered detrimental, like tobacco.

Social security—A federal program Americans pay into via FICA taxes during their working years and withdraw from when they retire. Elderly people and disabled people unable to work may collect social security funds.

Special Purpose Acquisition Company (SPAC)—A type of blank check company. A SPAC is an increasingly popular way for companies to become public.

Spending limit—The maximum balance one can charge to their credit card.

Stock—A share of ownership in a corporation.

Stock split—Occurs when a company increases the number of shares of its stock and proportionally decreases the share price. For example, an investor currently owns forty shares of a company that are trading at $70 each. The company announces a two-for-one stock split. As of the effective date, the investor owns eighty shares of the company at $35.

Taxable account—An investment account that does not have the tax advantages of accounts like an IRA, meaning an investor has to pay taxes on the account's investment earnings.

Ticker symbol—A string of characters that identifies a publicly traded company's shares.

Time horizon—The period an investor expects to hold a certain investment to meet a specific goal.

Time Value of Money (TVM)—A financial principle based on the idea that a dollar today is worth more than in the future because of the potential of compound interest.

Traditional IRA—A tax-advantaged retirement account. Pre-tax funds may be contributed to a traditional IRA, and funds are taxed upon withdrawal.

Valuation—The determination of a fair price for a security.

Volatility—The degree of movement in an asset's price.

Watch list—A list of investments an investor is interested in potentially purchasing. For example, an investor interested in investing in tech stocks might make a watch list with Alphabet, Apple, Microsoft, and Netflix.

W-2 form—A tax form issued by employers which outlines an employee's wages and taxes withheld from their paycheck throughout the year.

Acknowledgments

This book would not have been possible without the love and hard work of so many people. Thank you to everyone who has supported me from the beginning.

To my remarkable sister Maya, thank you for all the "emotional support," like when I asked you to keep it down when I was working on my book, and you turned the volume up instead.

Mom and Dad, thank you for your unconditional love and support and for teaching me what hard work looks like.

Infinite love and gratitude to my grandparents, Paul and Jyoti Khosla and Manak and Santosh Gupta.

I would like to extend a special thank you to Kara Caccuitto, Delia Follet, and Jamie Roszel for your guidance.

My deepest gratitude to Neale Godfrey for believing in me.

A huge thank you to my interviewees, who made this book possible:

Tiffany Aliche, Louis Barajas, Jennifer Barrett, Sahil Bloom, Chris Brown, Tim Chen, Jedidiah Collins, Kelly DiGonzini, Karen Finerman, JJ Kinahan, Kelly Lannan, Ben Martinek, Nate O'Brien, Andy Rachleff, Jill Schlesinger, Tim Sheehan, Andrew Ross Sorkin, Jonah Stillman, Tanya Van Court, and Lauryn Williams.

Last but not least, a heartfelt thank you to everyone whose support allowed me to bring this book into fruition:

Arun Aagarwal; Rajesh Abbi; Anya Abhayakumar; Sudhish K Aggarwal ; Asra Ali; Sumi Ariely; Eva, Neil, and Sheila Awasathi; Garima Bansil; Candra Bass; Lan Bello; Heidi Berman; Brooke Bevan; Brij, Devin, and Mira Bhatt; Elise Boyse; Deborah Boysen; Kathy Bratzke; Stephen Brisette; Madhu Chandak; Allie and Bela Chandler; Rajenda Chhabra; Patricia Edwards; Emma Esposito; Laura Gardner; Vipin Garg; Lisa Ghorbani; Danica Ginsberg; Gurmale Singh Grewal; Anoopum Gupta; Dilan, Kasmira, and Sarina Gupta; Jai, Nikki, and Suri Gupta; Nana Hans; Justin Hauser; Michael Winn Hauser; Tim Jordan; Eesha, Reena, and Rohan Kachhy; Yash Kataria; Anjana and Ashok Katyal; Eric Koester; Ravi Kohli; Ava Lathan; Andy Lutz; Manju Malkani; Carolyn, Corinne, and Vanessa May; Arian and Navya Mehrotra; Shailen and Simren Mehta; Abhishek Mishra; Bina and Chander Mohan; Alex, Katelyn, and Ryan Nagaraj; Anjali and Kavya Narahari; Kathleen Nissman; Hari Nath; Patrick Noonan; Kajal Parmar; Elise and Ronan Patel; Mila Patel; Silvina Pereira; Mohammed Rahman; Atif Raja; Ralph Ramos; Cy Reading; Charles H Robinson Jr; Alison, Aubry, and William Rogers; Teja Wasudev; Jignasa Sachar; Bharat Sareen; Mohan Sawhney; Matthew Schricker; Devin and

Nina Sehgal; Madhu Sethi; Saiyan, Sohaan, and Roshan Shah; Samantha Shah; Malu Singh; Kareena and Bayla Sheshadri; Naina Singla; Mangal Swaminathan; Nousha Tehrani; Morris Treadway; Margaret Ann Turnbull; Manoj Kumar Uppal; Michael Young; Hailey Zhang

Appendix

———

INTRODUCTION

Israel, Haim, Lauma Kalns-Timans, Martyn Briggs, Pinaki Das, Felix Tran, and Francesca Hanania. *"Thematic Investing; Ok Zoomer: Gen Z Primer.* Charlotte, North Carolina: Bank of America Corporation, 2020.

Stress in America: Generation Z. American Psychological Association, 2018.

Williams, Alex. "Move Over, Millennials, Here Comes Gen Z." *New York Times,* September 18, 2015. https://www.nytimes.com/2015/09/20/fashion/move-over-millennials-here-comes-generation-z.html.

CHAPTER 1

Anagnos, Chloe. "When It Comes to Money, Gen Z Is Way Ahead of Millennials." *Foundation for Economic Education*, February 25, 2020. https://fee.org/articles/when-it-comes-to-money-gen-z-is-way-ahead-of-millennials/.

Desjardins, Jeff. "Why Generation Z Has a Totally Different Approach to Money." *World Economic Forum,* November 30, 2018. https://www.weforum.org/agenda/2018/11/why-gen-z-is-approaching-money-differently-than-other-generations-95032cb6-6046-4269-a38a-0763bd7909ff/.

Gilchrist, Karen. "She Got Plastic Bags Banned on Bali by 18. Now She Wants to Mobilize Other Young Activists." *CNBC,* August 20, 2020. https://www.cnbc.com/2020/08/20/plastic-pollution-gen-z-activist-melati-wijsen-mobilizes-others.html

Greenlight Financial Technology, Inc. "Survey Finds Gen Z Lacks Knowledge in Personal Finance and Investing." Greenlight Financial Technology, Inc. press release, April 1, 2021.

Rosen, Steve. "Gen Z Not Eager to Take on Student Debt." *Chicago Tribune,* June 13, 2017. https://www.chicagotribune.com/business/success/tca-gen-z-not-eager-to-take-on-student-debt-20170613-story.html.

Olya, Gabrielle. "How Gen Z Plans to Avoid Student Loans." *Yahoo Finance*, December 3, 2020. https://www.yahoo.com/lifestyle/gen-z-plans-avoid-student-170026396.html.

Swain-Wilson, Savanna. "10 Ways Gen Zs Spend Money Differently Than Their Gen X Parents," *Insider,* November 28, 2018. https://www.insider.com/gen-z-vs-gen-x-spending-habits-2018-11#in-general-gen-xers-are-considered-deliberate-overspenders-while-gen-zers-are-cautious-savers-10.

The Vanguard Group, Inc. *Generational Views on Financial Advice, Investing, and Retirement.* Valley Forge, Pennsylvania: Vanguard Group, Inc., 2020.

Treger, Stan and Courey Gruszauskas. "Dispatches From Generation Z." *Morningstar,* June 2, 2020. https://www.morningstar.com/articles/986106/dispatches-from-generation-z.

CHAPTER 2

Pavia, Jim. "Mad Money's Jim Cramer Recalls 'Money Talks' With His Dad." *CNBC,* June 13, 2019. https://www.cnbc.com/2019/06/13/mad-moneys-jim-cramer-recalls-money-talks-with-his-dad.html.

CHAPTER 3

Anderson, Joel. "Survey Finds Most Common Reasons Americans Use Emergency Funds." *GoBankingRates,* May 24, 2018. https://www.gobankingrates.com/saving-money/budgeting/how-americans-use-emergency-fund/.

Haverty, Laura. "Surviving a Brain Aneurysm Taught Me This About Personal Finance." *NBC News,* April 26, 2019. https://www.nbcnews.com/know-your-value/feature/surviving-brain-aneurysm-taught-me-about-personal-finance-ncna998326.

Weliver, David. "Put Your Money on Autopilot." *Money Under 30,* April 17, 2019. https://www.moneyunder30.com/money-on-autopilot.

CHAPTER 4

Huddleston Jr., Tom. "How Warren Buffett Spends His Billions." *CNBC*, August 19, 2020. https://www.cnbc.com/2020/08/19/how-warren-buffett-spends-his-billions.html

Leonhardt, Megan. "64 percent of Americans Changed Their Spending Habits During the Pandemic—Here's How." *CNBC*, September 29, 2020. https://www.cnbc.com/2020/09/29/americans-have-changed-their-spending-habits-during-the-pandemic-heres-how.html

O'Connell, Jodi. "5 of Warren Buffett's Most Frugal Habits." *Business Insider,* May 21, 2017. https://www.businessinsider.com/5-of-warren-buffetts-most-frugal-habits-2017-5#buffett-treats-his-friends-well-but-not-extravagantly-5

Smith, Jodie. "Money-Saving Teen Jordon Cox: From Blogging to Berlin." *BBC News*, February 6, 2016. https://www.bbc.com/news/uk-england-essex-35482102.

Wong, Danny. "What Science Says About Discounts, Promotions and Free Offers." *Huffington Post,* November 10, 2015. https://www.huffpost.com/entry/what-science-says-about-discounts_b_8511224

CHAPTER 5

Anna Bessendorf. *From Cradle to Cane: The Cost of Being a Female Consumer.* New York City, New York: New York City Department of Consumer Affairs, 2015.

Carbon Tax Center. "What's a Carbon Tax?" https://www.carbon-tax.org/whats-a-carbon-tax/.

Hess, Abigail Johnson. "College Grads Expect to Earn $60,000 in Their First Job—Here's How Much They Actually Make." *CNBC*, February 17, 2019. https://www.cnbc.com/2019/02/15/college-grads-expect-to-earn-60000-in-their-first-job----few-do.html.

Kagan, Julia. "Luxury Tax." *Investopedia,* updated July 19, 2020. https://www.investopedia.com/terms/l/luxury_tax.asp#:~:text=A%20luxury%20tax%20is%20a,amount%20above%20a%20specified%20level.

Orem, Tina. "2020-2021 Tax Brackets and Federal Income Tax Rates." Nerdwallet, April 12, 2021. https://www.nerdwallet.com/article/taxes/federal-income-tax-bracketshttps://www.nerdwallet.com/article/taxes/federal-income-tax-brackets.

Tax Foundation. "Independence Day: Taxes Then and Now." https://taxfoundation.org/independence-day-taxes-then-and-now/.

CHAPTER 6

Graham, Luke. "10 Expensively Insured Body Parts." *CNBC*, September 9, 2016. https://www.cnbc.com/2016/09/09/10-expensively-insured-body-parts.html

CHAPTER 7

Zweig, Jason. "Warren Buffett and the $300,000 Haircut." *The Wall Street Journal,* August 28, 2020. https://www.wsj.com/articles/warren-buffett-and-the-300-000-haircut-11598626805

CHAPTER 8

Sheng, Ellen. "Coronavirus Crisis Mobile Banking Surge is a Shift That's Likely to Stick." *CNBC,* May 27, 2020. https://www.cnbc.com/2020/05/27/coronavirus-crisis-mobile-banking-surge-is-a-shift-likely-to-stick.html

CHAPTER 9

myFico. "Loan Savings Calculator." https://www.myfico.com/credit-education/calculators/loan-savings-calculator/.

myFico. "How are FICO Scores Calculated?" https://www.myfico.com/credit-education/whats-in-your-credit-score.

CHAPTER 10

Csiszar, John. "How Much You Take Home from the Average Salary in Each State." *Yahoo Finance,* October 13, 2020. https://finance.yahoo.com/news/much-really-home-average-salary-090000412.html.

Glassman, James. "An Old Lady's Lesson: Patience Usually Pays." *Washington Post,* December 17, 1995. https://www.washingtonpost.com/archive/business/1995/12/17/an-old-ladys-lesson-patience-usually-pays/ec000053-d7bf-4014-b841-546bd5847a80/.

Martin, Emmie. "If You Invested $1,000 in Apple at Its IPO, Here's How Much Money You'd Have Now." *CNBC,* November 1, 2018. https://www.cnbc.com/2018/11/01/how-much-a-1000-dollar-investment-in-apple-at-its-ipo-would-be-worth-now.html.

US Bureau of Labor Statistics. "CPI Inflation Calculator." https://www.bls.gov/data/inflation_calculator.htm.

CHAPTER 11

Jackson, Anna-Louise. "Warren Buffett: 'for Most People, the Best Thing' Is to Own This Kind of Index Fund." *Grow,* updated October 12, 2020. https://grow.acorns.com/warren-buffett-index-funds/.

CHAPTER 15

Bernhardt, Donald, Marshall Eckblad, and Federal Reserve Bank of Chicago. "Stock Market Crash of 1987." Federal Reserve History, November 22, 2013. https://www.federalreservehistory.org/essays/stock_market_crash_of_1987.

Domm, Patti. "How the Pandemic Drove Massive Stock Market Gains, and What Happens Next." *CNBC,* December 30, 2020. https://www.cnbc.com/2020/12/30/how-the-pandemic-drove-massive-stock-market-gains-and-what-happens-next.html.

Halton, Clay. "Black Tuesday." *Investopedia,* updated January 9, 2021. https://www.investopedia.com/terms/b/blacktuesday.asp.

Hayes, Adam. "Dotcom Bubble." *Investopedia,* updated June 25, 2019. https://www.investopedia.com/terms/d/dotcom-bubble.asp.

Hulbert, Mark. "25 Years to Bounce Back? Try 4 1/2." *New York Times,* April 25, 2009. https://www.nytimes.com/2009/04/26/your-money/stocks-and-bonds/26stra.html.

Zarroli, Jim. "Stocks 2020: A Stunning Crash, Then A Record Boom Created Centibillionaires." *NPR,* December 31, 2020. https://www.npr.org/2020/12/31/952267894/stocks-2020-a-stunning-crash-then-a-record-setting-boom-created-centi-billionaire.

Time, Not Timing, is the Best Way to Capitalize on Stock Market Gains. Boston, Massachusetts: Putnam Investments.

CHAPTER 16

Apple Inc. "Apple Commits to Be 100 Percent Carbon Neutral for Its Supply Chain and Products by 2030." Apple Inc. press release, July 21, 2020. Apple Inc. website. https://www.apple.com/newsroom/2020/07/apple-commits-to-be-100-percent-carbon-neutral-for-its-supply-chain-and-products-by-2030/, accessed October 6, 2020.

Bank of America Securities. *10 Reasons to Care about Environmental, Social and Governance (ESG) Investing.* Charlotte, North Carolina: Bank of America Corporation, 2020.

Hale, Jon. "Sustainable Equity Funds Outperform Traditional Peers in 2020." *Morningstar,* January 8, 2021. https://www.morningstar.com/articles/1017056/sustainable-equity-funds-outperform-traditional-peers-in-2020.

Liu, Jess. "ESG Investing Comes of Age." *Morningstar,* February 11, 2020. https://www.morningstar.com/features/esg-investing-history.

Microsoft Corporation. "Corporate Social Responsibility." Accessed October 6, 2020. https://www.microsoft.com/en-us/corporate-responsibility.

Morgan Stanley Institute for Sustainable Investing. *Sustainable Signals: Individual Investor Interest Driven by Impact, Conviction and Choice.* New York, New York: Morgan Stanley & Co. LLC and Morgan Stanley Smith Barney LLC, 2019.

MSCI. "Volkswagen Scandal Underlines Need for ESG Analysis." Accessed August 30, 2020. https://www.msci.com/volkswagen-scandal.

Stevens, Pippa. "Your Complete Guide to Investing with a Conscience, a $30 Trillion Market Just Getting Started." *CNBC,* December 14, 2019. https://www.cnbc.com/2019/12/14/your-complete-guide-to-socially-responsible-investing.html.

The Vanguard Group, Inc. "ESG Investing: Discover Funds That Reflect What Matters Most to You." Accessed August 29, 2020. https://investor.vanguard.com/investing/esg/.

CHAPTER 17

Acorns. https://www.acorns.com/.

Public.com. "Features." https://public.com/features.

Robinhood. https://robinhood.com/us/en/.

Wile, Rob. "Back In The Day, Brokers Got Away With Murder in Trading Commissions." *Business Insider,* March 31, 2014. https://www.businessinsider.com/historical-trading-commissions-2014-3.

CHAPTER 18

Apple. "Apple Pay." https://www.apple.com/apple-pay/.

Google Pay. "About Google Pay." https://pay.google.com/about/.

Toplin, Jaime. "Banking & Payments for Gen Z Report: The Winning Strategies for Attracting the Next Big Opportunity—Generation Z." *Business Insider,* May 1, 2019. https://www.businessinsider.com/banking-and-payments-for-gen-z.

Treger, Stan and Courey Gruszauskas. "Dispatches From Generation Z." *Morningstar,* June 2, 2020. https://www.morningstar.com/articles/986106/dispatches-from-generation-z.

BONUS

Browne, Ryan. "Burger King Has Launched Its Own Cryptocurrency in Russia Called 'WhopperCoin.'" *CNBC,* August 28, 2017. https://www.cnbc.com/2017/08/28/burger-king-russia-cryptocurrency-whoppercoin.html.

Browne, Ryan. "IBM Partners with Nestle, Unilever and Other Food Giants to Trace Food Contamination with Blockchain." *CNBC,* August 22, 2017. https://www.cnbc.com/2017/08/22/

ibm-nestle-unilever-walmart-blockchain-food-contamination.html.

Browne, Ryan. "UK Hospitals Are Using Blockchain to Track the Temperature of Coronavirus Vaccines." *CNBC,* January 19, 2021. https://www.cnbc.com/2021/01/19/uk-hospitals-use-blockchain-to-track-coronavirus-vaccine-temperature.html.

Goldstein, Jacob. *Money: The True story of a Made-Up Thing.* New York: Hachette Books, 2020.

Kratter, Matthew. *A Beginner's Guide to Bitcoin.*

Made in the USA
Columbia, SC
03 June 2022

61297708R00176